What Others Are Saying
and *Family Pray*

"We all know that prayer changes things, and that when we pray together in unity, heaven hears and moves on our behalf. Teresa Herbic has done all of the legwork for us with her prayer guide in order that we might pray as families. I can't think of anything more powerful or more important. This book will bless you and anchor your home. I highly recommend it."

—*Terry Meeuwsen*
Co-host, *700 Club*
Director, Orphan's Promise

"It was my privilege to be Teresa and her family's pastor during many challenging times of adopting their children, praying for healing, and seeking wisdom as parents. We saw the hand of God and the faithfulness of Teresa's prayer at work. You will be greatly inspired by the stories included here and the practical help that comes from someone who passionately practices and encourages authentic prayer."

—*Vernon Armitage*
Pastor, Briarcliff Church
Teacher, Willow Creek Community Church
Co-author, *Living Life to the Max*

"Teresa's love of her family and commitment to following God's call unite beautifully in this powerful guide to growing closer to God with your family through prayer. Throughout her orphan advocacy work, Teresa has inspired others to be bold in their compassion and faith. It's such a blessing that through *Family Prayer Made Easy*, Teresa is able to share these important principles with the world!"

—*Hollen Frazier*
President, All God's Children International

"Wow! Teresa delivers a book that so many families can actually use to re-connect to God. In our fast-paced, busy world, even the most faithful may not make time to pause for prayer. *Family Prayer Made Easy* makes daily prayer a fun, family activity while keeping the faith. Teresa's lifelong dedication to orphans—both children and animals—is unwavering, and she consistently finds ways to celebrate and nurture God in our everyday lives. That love and passion for God shines brightly in this guide. A wonderful resource to jumpstart daily prayer for all family members—parents and kids alike."

—*Karen L. Allanach*
Communications manager, Faith Outreach & Engagement
The Humane Society of the United States

"Teresa Herbic loves the Lord, loves families, and loves children (particularly those in need of a 'forever family' through foster or adoptive placement). Her love shines through this book as she writes about new and creative ways to share the truth and good news of the gospel with those for whom she so deeply cares."

—*Dr. Robert C. Springate*
Vice president, Missouri Baptist Children's Home Foundation

"Families are forever. Teresa brings to life the ministry of family. In this insightful guide, she shares how together we build forever families."

—*Dave Coffman*
Director, Adoption Resource Foundation

"Ephesians 6:18 encourages us to pray in the Spirit on all occasions. This book gives practical ways to do just that. Teresa has a passion for Christ and for families. She and her husband Galen have endured much to help others as they pursue God's calling to build up the family unit. I pray readers imitate this as they learn from the dynamic words shared in this book."

—*Greg Blankenship*
Lead pastor, Real Life Corpus, Corpus Christi, Texas

"Teresa Herbic and her family have been good friends over the years, and I know all of them to be praying people, as well as a praying family. They believe wholeheartedly in the power of prayer, and I have seen prayer work for them in their own lives. They have seen its results. I have no doubt that Teresa's biblical ideas presented in this book will bring results in other families' lives as well. She can be trusted to give good advice! I heartily endorse and recommend this book to you!"

—*Emil Bartos*
Pastor, Peace Lutheran Church, Hollister, Missouri

"I first became acquainted with Teresa many years ago in a prayer group that met every Wednesday night. From the beginning it was obvious that she had a passion for prayer and for helping orphan children. Her passion went beyond seeing hurting children and praying for them. She put actions to her desires. Teresa Herbic will always be at the top of my list when ministering to orphaned or foster children and their families or potential families. She prays boldly about all that she does."

—*Patricia Raines*
Retired family ministry assistant, Pleasant Valley Baptist Church

"I have known Teresa Herbic's transparent heart for years as we have prayed for one another and for other prayer warriors worldwide. Teresa is a sacred prayer partner, friend, and sweet spirit."

—*Susie Carter*
Prayer partner

"Teresa's message about God's special children flows from her heart of inspiration, wisdom, and experience. Teresa is an impassioned advocate for His special children and hopeful parents."

—*Cheri McCoy*
Author, *Pieces of My Heart*

"I have known Teresa for over ten years, and we have worked together to create a support group to bring our children together, all of whom are adopted. In that time, she has shown leadership, a creative mind, an intuition of what will work, and a heartfelt passion for prayer and for families and children around the world. Through all of that, her devotion to the One who brought all of this together, Jesus Christ our Lord and Savior, is what really drives her."

—*Angie Pollock*
Cofounder, Families for Adoption, Pleasant Valley Baptist Church

"Prayer is the vital fabric that weaves families together. The youngest of eight children, I grew up in a family that lived and taught us these same valuable truths that Teresa teaches. We literally prayed out loud every day—for safety, for the passing ambulance, for our food, and so on. Years later, when my life was shattered by the sudden deaths of my wife and of all four of our children, only the grace of almighty God and the power of prayer brought me through. To live a life with no regrets with your family, heed these compelling words from Teresa Herbic contained within the covers of this powerful book. You'll never regret it."

—*Robert Rogers*
Founder, Mighty in the Land Ministry
Speaker, Songwriter
Author, *Into the Deep, 7 Steps to No Regrets,* and *Rise Above*

FAMILY
PRAYER
Made Easy

TERESA J. HERBIC

WHITAKER
HOUSE

FAMILY PRAYER MADE EASY:
A Practical Guide for Praying Together

Teresa J. Herbic
familiesforadoption@gmail.com

ISBN: 978-1-62911-738-6
eBook ISBN: 978-1-62911-739-3
Printed in the United States of America
© 2016 by Teresa J. Herbic

Whitaker House
1030 Hunt Valley Circle
New Kensington, PA 15068
www.whitakerhouse.com

Library of Congress Cataloging-in-Publication Data

Names: Herbic, Teresa J., 1968- author.
Title: Family prayer made easy : a practical guide for praying together / by Teresa J. Herbic.
Description: New Kensington, PA : Whitaker House, [2016]
Identifiers: LCCN 2016026714 (print) | LCCN 2016028588 (ebook) | ISBN 9781629117386 (trade pbk. : alk. paper) | ISBN 9781629117393 (ebook)
Subjects: LCSH: Families--Prayers and devotions.
Classification: LCC BV255 .H455 2016 (print) | LCC BV255 (ebook) | DDC 249--dc23
LC record available at https://lccn.loc.gov/2016026714

1 2 3 4 5 6 7 8 9 10 11 ᴜᴜ 23 22 21 20 19 18 17 16

to my sacred prayer circle—my family

Personal Commitment to Prayer

We acknowledge our personal agreement to unite in prayer as a family, to remain together through good times and bad, and to ensure God is the center of our family life. We will meet _____ (daily or weekly) at the time _____ to pray.

_____
(Dad's signature)

_____
(Mom's signature)

_____
(Guardian's signature)

_____
(Child's signature)

_____
(Child's signature)

_____
(Child's signature)

_____
(Child's signature)

_____
(Child's signature)

Signed this _____ day of _____, _____
               Day   Month   Year

CONTENTS

Foreword...11

Introduction..14

Devotional 1:   Praying for a Happy Family......................21

Devotional 2:   Praying for Our Friends 30

Devotional 3:   Praying for Our Salvation and
                Our Church..37

Devotional 4:   Praying for Students, Schools,
                and Teachers 45

Devotional 5:   Praying at Mealtimes.............................52

Devotional 6:   Praying for Our Safety, Sleep,
                and Security 57

Devotional 7:   Praying for Our World, Nation,
                and Community 64

Devotional 8:   Praying for Those Who Are Sick.............71

Devotional 9:   Praying During Grief and Hardship 79

Devotional 10: Praying about Serving God.....................86

100 More Simple Ideas for Family or Group Prayer 93

Prayers for Holidays and Special Occasions 119

What God Says About Prayer 145

Classic Children's Prayers 150

Conclusion: Father's Love Letter 162

Appendix: Prayer Resources 167

Acknowledgments 174

About the Author 175

FOREWORD

Whether you're reading through the entire book or dipping in for an idea for family time, you will spark a flame of purposeful, focused prayer by opening these pages. And the flame won't flicker out! This book is an ongoing guide to promoting perseverance in prayer.

I've witnessed this perseverance personally in the life of the author, Teresa. When I first met the young couple joining our church prayer group, I sensed a vibrancy in them that shone with the love of Jesus. *Love* is the "action word" lived out by Teresa and Galen every day. Both as a couple and as individuals, their lives and prayers demonstrate a genuine faith. Teresa prays with mighty faith knowing she can completely trust our Lord to act in love, and Galen has a humble heart that opens the heavens for his prayers to enter into the Holy of Holies.

They both pour their hearts out daily in love to the Lord God and allow God's love to pour out toward others. They taught me, by their examples, how to be an open vessel of God's true love.

Their faith really took flight when Galen and Teresa traveled internationally to adopt Meyana and, later, Braxten. Our prayer group and dedicated prayer partners lifted them up to Abba for

Him to make a way for their two children to be adopted. "Prayer first" has always been modeled by the Herbics. They put faith and love in action by overcoming every obstacle in Jesus' strength to bring their children home. Through both the joys and the intense trials, they have poured their hearts and lives into raising Meyana and Braxten in the truth of the gospel.

Their love of the Lord now flows into the hearts of their children, who then share the love with others. Witnessing their children already living out faith in God is a gift to them and to all of us who know them. The Herbic family is God's chosen instrument; they effectively serve others in loving-kindness with boldness. It is contagious and energizing for the people in their lives—including me!

Prayer, Bible reading, and worship so obviously ignite the love they share transparently with others. Jesus Christ is the Cornerstone of their home, and the Holy Spirit fills them as they pray. We've witnessed answer after answer come to their prayers, to the glory of the Lord. Not only that, but fruit is evident and abundant in their Christian faith journey. Love, joy, peace, patience, kindness, goodness, gentleness, faithfulness, and self-control thrive in their lives.

And this book is filled with that fruit. Teresa's willingness to share her family's prayer lifestyle will inspire readers to look inside their own hearts. At the same time, Teresa's drive for compassion will inspire readers to learn how to pray for the hurting, lost, lonely, and suffering in all walks of life.

Teresa's writing allows many to grow in the knowledge of living for Jesus daily, and I am confident that her wisdom on prayer will benefit families and people of all ages. The fingerprints of our heavenly Father can be seen all over this book in its unique, powerful, expressive prayer ideas. Teresa recognizes children relate to God in a wide variety of creative ways, and so she crafted this book to be adaptable. Each idea, however, has one goal: to unite families to God and to each other. This book encourages relationship-building that is both vertical, toward the Lord, and horizontal, with family members and friends.

Keeping a consistent prayer life is difficult for every family, but this book shows how to start a family prayer time and keep the fire of prayer burning. Its Scripture references align readers' prayers with God's will and draw readers into God's holy Word.

I wish everyone would read this book! If they did, communities would be mightily impacted by God's answering of prayers. Churches would be stronger, functioning as the body of Christ and fostering growth in acts of loving-kindness to each other and the communities. Marriages would be restored as couples lead their children in persevering prayer. Restoration, healing, wholeness in Christ Jesus, solidarity in God's purposes, and love in action would be evident.

That's what I'm praying for!

—*Sandy Glasgow*
Global outreach prayer coordinator,
Pleasant Valley Baptist Church
Liberty, Missouri

INTRODUCTION

Today's families are busy. We sprint off in the morning to school, work, music lessons, sports, and other activities. We return home, often tuning in to television, computers, and technology—and tuning each other out! For many of us, social media has taken over the free minutes, resulting in less communication and more screen time.

What would be the "dream activity" you'd do with your family, if your schedule allowed it? Depending on the season, maybe you envision a picnic in the park, having a nice dinner around the table, going on a hayride, or adventuring together to choose a Christmas tree or pumpkin. One of my earliest memories of my family is us just sitting together on the grassy front lawn of our home in the country, sipping iced tea and talking about our day. Sure, that may seem boring to some, but it stuck with me all these years. Why? Because we were connecting—feeling meaningful love and enjoyment with family. I never forgot it.

What would happen to your family if you paused to regain true connection? What if you took quality time to seek the highest measure of joy, peace, help, and assurance available—God's love and answers through prayer? As Acts 17:27–28 says, we need to *"seek him and perhaps reach out for him and find him, though he is not far from any one of* us. 'For in him we live and move and have our being'" (NIV). It's clear: time in prayer offers direct access to God's heart. It offers connection with Him—and a deeper, more meaningful connection with each other.

And it can be as simple as sitting together on a lawn.

Family Prayer Made Easy is a guide for growing together through prayer in just ten focused devotionals with optional activities. Together, you and your family will pursue God in Spirit-driven, action-packed, answer-delivering prayers. Whether you meet once a week for ten weeks or ten straight days, it's completely up to you, but its prayer activities will impact your life.

My Story

As parents, it's our duty to teach our children not to be worried, ashamed, or afraid, but in everything to seek God, who can move and help us. The more this is instilled in our being at a young age, the stronger our faith and joy in Christ will mature.

Now, please don't think that our family is perfect. Our family, like most, has suffered through the trenches. Yet, it is often in the trenches that we learn He is at work in miraculous ways in our family. This was brought home to me through the blindness of our dear adopted daughter, Meyana.

Meyana was legally blind—20/2400—when we adopted her at age twelve months, but we didn't realize it at first. As she grew older, we kept noticing her rubbing her eyes. She began telling us, "It's so blurry." We took her to the optometrist for a diagnosis, and were shocked and distraught at the diagnosis. We requested the intervention of doctors. We patched her good eye for more than a year. Then, she had a disastrous surgery leaving her with double vision and extensive vision issues for years. We sought guidance from six doctors. Meyana endured eye patches, special vision glasses, and years of therapy, but nothing seemed to improve.

What proved persistent and increasing, however, was Meyana's faith. Saved at an early age, she trusted the Lord wholeheartedly. She told me often, "Mom, Jesus is the only doctor I really need." Along with our pastors and fellow believers, we pleaded to God for a breakthrough. We felt desperate. One night a program came on TV about a specialist treating a boy who had double vision, like Meyana, and was about the same age as Meyana, too. The boy was healed. We knew we must find this doctor.

With the support of many friends, church members, and family, we traveled to UCLA to meet the specialist. Initially, he planned to conduct surgery only on the left eye but later told us that he needed to operate on both. We felt confident that it was all in God's hands. Pleading on our hands and knees for a miracle in a stark, crowded waiting room, we believed in nothing short of a manifestation of His power and glory. We prayed *"For nothing will be impossible with God"* (Luke 1:37) over and over and over.

Meyana woke up in recovery with two extremely bloody, swollen, nearly-shut eyes. We breathlessly asked what she could see—and she quietly responded that she still saw everything in double. Drowning in disbelief, I cried uncontrollably, thinking God had let me down.

God, however, wasn't quite finished. Despite her pain, Meyana noticed a splendid rainbow outside the window. She could see what I couldn't with 20/20 sight: God's power and love beamed through into the hospital room. She said, "We have to keep faith in God. Maybe it's just going to take a little longer."

At the follow-up appointment, the doctor altered lenses and prisms over Meyana's eyes. She saw a single picture for the first time, even if for a mere second. It was remarkable! A few weeks later, Meyana asked if she could read the Lord's Prayer. She began reading the passage. Then suddenly, she exclaimed, "I can see! I can see one picture!" The double vision had healed. To this day, it has never returned. Praise God in all of His glory!

Stories from Our Friends

Today, we appreciate that through trials, faith, and obedience God has the capacity to heal anyone, anytime, and to change any situation. He can bless any family as long as they pray and seek Him in an unwavering, humble, and authentic way. After all, God knows our hearts and our minds—He knows what we're thinking. Sharing from the core of our souls with the Father who made us and loves us are key ingredients to a prayerful life. We put ourselves out there, sharing in honesty, hope, and love, and God presents His blessings back to us according to His riches and glory.

And we're not the only ones. Our friends Michael and Kimber Daniels' deepest desire was to permanently adopt little Shaye from foster care, but they faced major obstacles. Still, the night before their court hearing, in an aisle in Walgreen's, we locked eyes and determined we should pray together. We are all family in Christ. God can do this, we agreed. It's our duty to seek Him. We prayed. The next day, the adoption of Shaye became official.

And there's the Easons. The mom, Susan, had always hoped for a sibling for her daughter, Jade. Susan found out that little Matt was available for international adoption through an agency and shared the possibility with Jade. Although Jade had her heart set on a sister, they prayed together and afterward, Jade agreed it was fine to have a brother. She even began "missing" Matt as soon as she learned he would be her sibling. Every time she said she missed him, Susan and Jade would pray together—for Matt, for Jesus' protection of Matt, and for healing of Matt's hearing disability. A few weeks later, when she received approval to adopt Matt, Susan received an e-mail from his orphanage: his hearing disability had disappeared! When Matt came home, Susan felt blessed to have two adopted children who adored each other.

But anxiety struck again when Matt failed a few hearing tests. Instead of being alarmed, however, they sought the Lord in prayer and visited an ENT. It was then decided he should undergo a surgery fairly common for young children. Now, Matt has perfect hearing. Praise God for the way He moves and continues to work out all the details!

Prayer Works!

I share these stories to let you know that miraculous answers to prayer do happen to those who pray daily with their families. And that's not just my opinion. One of the greatest promises on prayer is found in Matthew 18:19: *"If two of you agree on earth about anything they ask, it will be done for them by my Father in heaven."* (You can find so many more promises about prayer in "What God Says About Prayer," page 145.)

That sounds great, doesn't it? But how do we actually do that?

In only ten steps, this book's prayer action plan will teach your family to pray more deeply. There are over one hundred prayer activities that are simple methods to grow more in tune with God. There's much more to life than living in chaos, crowded schedules, and desperation! Instead, by praising God and working actively in our lives to meet with Him in our daily schedule, we can bring joy and purpose to our routine. We can grow fond of God's Word which comforts us as we pray. We can learn to appreciate God's promises as reality, not just pipe dreams. That's the power of God and His strength in family!

How to Use This Book

Each devotional in the book follows this pattern:

+ **Family Minute:** Gather your family and read the family devotion aloud. It includes a brief opening prayer, a Scripture, and a short, true story from my life. Then, read the questions aloud that follow the story, and answer them openly and honestly. As appropriate, read aloud the simple encouragements included in italics after the questions.

Next, read aloud the simple prayer. Offering an example of prayer is an easy way to teach children to pray. (Remind children that they can pray anytime and not just as a family—they can pray alone, too! Whether it's in their rooms, at school, or wherever it may be, they should pray in pure silence from their hearts and souls as they feel comfortable or are led.)

Then, read aloud the Scriptures. You can have children bring their own Bibles and look up the references, taking turns to be the one reading aloud. Consider choosing one Scripture to memorize together. God's promises on the topic at hand are included for your encouragement and to share with your family if time allows.

+ **Interactive Family Prayer:** There are two or more options to choose from. Pick the one that best fits your family, and jump in—together!

+ **Community Activity:** There is also an optional community prayer activity for those involved in small community or support groups.

After the ten topics for prayer, there's a chapter of one hundred more family and group prayer activities to keep you seeking and discovering.

Ten Steps to Fruitful Prayer

Before you dive in to rejuvenating your family prayer life, take a moment to review the following ten key steps to fruitful prayer:

1. Determine what answer you hope to gain in prayer.

2. Find a Scripture that will support the prayer (Scriptures are listed in each chapter to help you).

3.   Praise and give thanks to God for the opportunity to pray for His answer.

4.   Petition (ask) God for the answer with all your heart, mind, and soul. This book encourages not only family prayer together, but also intimate personal prayer and communication with God. You can pray as a group, alone, or however you wish, as long as you are seeking the Father.

5.   Make every prayer be one of pure faith, refusing to doubt God's ability to answer.

Rely on God in full confidence that He can and will answer.

6.   Lift the Scripture to God as His Word and promise.

7.   Thank God for hearing your prayer.

8.   Trust God in gladness and assurance that He will answer if it is His will.

9.   Then, worship and praise God for working on your behalf to deliver His answer.

10. Once an answer is delivered, give God the glory for all He has done in your family life.

Do you desire a closer bond with God? Then don't wait! Just follow the step-by-step guide. You can do a devotional a day for ten days, or a devotional a week for ten weeks. Either way, your success depends on your continued participation in this simple process. Now, journey forth. Don't let anything stop you!

The impact you desire begins *now*!

Let's uncover God's influence, power, and glory together through your core prayer circle—your family. May your family be blessed as you uncover God's hope, joy, perseverance, power, plan, and truth. And remember as you read, I'm thanking Jesus for you! Enjoy!

—*Teresa J. Herbic*

DEVOTIONAL 1:
PRAYING FOR A HAPPY FAMILY

Family Minute

Dear God, We praise You, and we seek You. We come before You as a family to ask for Your incredible answers—nothing less—because You are a God of everything wonderful! Amen.

If two of you agree on earth about anything they ask, it will be done for them by my Father in heaven. (Matthew 18:19)

True Story from Teresa

For years, my family and I attended a midweek prayer meeting at church. While my husband and I prayed with other parents, our kids joined Awana. It became our routine for years. Then, one day, our prayer group suddenly dissolved. We no longer had our sacred circle. We missed gathering with brothers and sisters to share our deepest heart matters. God had revealed great answers to us when we bared our souls to one another—but now we felt at a loss.

Then a dawn of light came over us: why not hold our own family prayer meetings?

Now our family—me, my husband, and our two kids—gather after dinner every Wednesday evening. Each person brings a Scripture with thoughts of concern or praise. When she was little, our daughter took this so seriously that she created paper programs, copying the ones she saw at church services. Our son even passed out programs at the doorway to our living room, exclaiming, "Welcome to family prayer night!"

Lifting our prayers, in the love of family, with the help of pastors and church friends, we saw awe-inspiring miracles at work regularly by the holy hand of God through our family prayer time. Not only that, but we also grew closer to each other by giving up time from our evening to worship as a family.

Questions and Thoughts

1. As family, do we have a regular, daily routine?

Maybe you get up, brush your teeth, comb your hair, have breakfast, and head out for the day.

2. When, during that routine, is a good time to stop and pray?

We have all been guilty of flying through the day and nearly forgetting to stop and thank our Creator who made us. The desire to pray comes from a genuine longing to draw closer to God and to know Him. Praying can become part of your daily routine. Ideally, it's great to start your day with prayer, but it's also helpful to pray midday, at night, or any time you can. However, it absolutely requires a firm commitment to make it happen.

3. How can this book help us?

Through this guide, you can begin to pray more deeply as a family. But it will take a commitment—from everybody! Determine a time that works for everyone to sit down together in a circle and do the simple activities to get started. Maybe you can meet daily after dinner or an hour before bedtime, but whatever you decide, remember that any time is a great time to pray! Then, sign together the "Personal Commitment to Prayer" at the beginning of this book if desired.

4. Do we have frustrations or needs as a family that require God's help and wisdom? Big or small, what prayer requests do we have?

The apostle Paul once said, "Don't worry about anything; instead pray about everything. Tell God what you need, and thank him for all he has done. Then you will experience God's peace, which exceeds anything we can understand. His peace will guard your hearts and minds as you live in Christ Jesus" *(Philippians 4:6–7* NLT*). If you lift your prayers, with the help of your inner circle of family, you are sure to see God's holy hand at work in your lives. But don't just pray when there's trouble. Take charge and pray and praise in all occasions. Then you will see God moving more boldly in your lives.*

A Simple Prayer

Dear Heavenly Father,

Thank You that You are our God. Thank You for loving our family. We love You! Dear God, please be at the center of our family as we move forward in prayer before You. Help us, Lord, to be a happy family. Bless our home with peace and love. Please bless each person by reminding us how to love each other as You love us. Help us to do our best each day to support one another, and not tear one another down. May our words to each other be gracious. Help us to know how we can serve You better. Thank You most of all that You made our family. We pray that You will guide us, help us, and protect us in all we do. We pray specifically for [family prayer requests]. In Jesus' holy name, we pray! Amen.

Scripture about Loving One Another:

(Read through together; consider memorizing one.)

This is my commandment, that you love one another as I have loved you.   (John 15:12)

Children, obey your parents in everything, for this pleases the Lord.   (Colossians 3:20)

Therefore, confess your sins to one another and pray for one another, that you may be healed. The prayer of a righteous person has great power as it is working.   (James 5:16)

Love is patient, love is kind. It does not envy, it does not boast, it is not proud. It does not dishonor others, it is not self-seeking, it is not easily angered, and it keeps no record of wrongs. Love does not delight in evil but rejoices with the truth. It always protects, always trusts, always hopes, always perseveres.
(1 Corinthians 13:4–7 NIV)

Therefore encourage one another and build one another up, just as you are doing.   (1 Thessalonians 5:11)

God's Promises

If any of you lacks wisdom, let him ask God, who gives generously to all without reproach, and it will be given him.
(James 1:5)

But know that the Lord has set apart the godly for himself; the Lord hears when I call to him.   (Psalm 4:3)

Surely goodness and mercy shall follow me all the days of my life, and I shall dwell in the house of the LORD forever.
(Psalm 23:6)

Trust in the LORD *with all your heart, and do not lean on your own understanding. In all your ways acknowledge him, and he will make straight your paths.*   (Proverbs 3:5–6)

Interactive Family Prayer

Option A: Hold a Candlelit Prayer Evening

Make a candlelit prayer evening special by handing out written invitations to each family member—whether they're adults, kids, or even toddlers. Include a specific day and time for the meeting. Ask them to bring one prayer request or thanksgiving to pray about.

A helpful format to follow in prayer is: praise, thanksgiving, confession, petition, closing prayer. Begin the night by praising God and offering thanks to Him. Tell Him how much you love Him and appreciate all He does for your family. Then, move into a time of confession.

Ask each person to contribute to every part of the prayer as they feel comfortable and let them know they can pray out loud or, if they prefer, silently. The goal is to make family members feel comfortable. Start by going around the room listing areas of concern. Then possibly play a worship song, a family-favorite hymn, or sing together in unison something simple. Move into thanksgiving for how the Lord has blessed your family, confession, and then petition for the prayer requests.

Close by saying a special prayer for your family harmony and your plan to pray more frequently together and give thanks to God for working in your lives.

Option B: Make Prayer Sticks for Long-Term Prayers

These prayer sticks are a simple, crafty way to remember to pray for long-term requests of those you love, such as salvation, addictions, family goals, and personal goals, hopes, or dreams.

1. Find, or purchase from a local crafting store, several Popsicle sticks per family member.

2. Have each person add special colors or design to the upper part of their sticks. Wind string, yarn, or colored cord around a section of the sticks. Alternatively—or in addition—you can paint bands of color on the sticks. For the least messy option, wrap with colored tape. You might even draw a cross to signify this is a prayer stick for Christ.

3. Next, write with a permanent marker the name or subject you want to pray for or about regularly on the base of each stick.

4. Choose or decorate a distinctive container or bowl to hold your prayer sticks. After you've made several of them, sit in a circle and hold a kick-off prayer time as you each draw out a stick one by one from the prayer container or bowl. Thank God for what He's about to do at the end of the prayer time, as He's bound to move and bless in the midst of such a loving family.

5. The first day of the month or first Sunday of the month, visit this container as a family and take turns pulling out a stick and praying about that subject or person.

6. Once a prayer is answered, remove that stick and either throw it away or keep it in an answered prayer box to reflect upon at the end of the year or even in later years as a family thanksgiving activity.

Option C: Love Letter to God—"Dad":

Read the following "Love Letter from God" shared with us by Deborah Ann Belka—a wonderful author from Faith Writers—to be included in this activity. Take turns reading or designate one person to read aloud.

Love Letter from God
By Deborah Ann Belka [1]

Today I received,
   A love letter from God.
I opened up my Bible
   Here is what I read…
I am your Creator,
   Before you were born;
I molded and formed you,
   Just like the dew in the morn.
I'm the remedy to your needs,
   I am your soothing balm,
I'm the peace in your storm,
   I am the voice that is calm.
I'm all the grace you need,
   In Me, there is eternal life.
I came so that I could bear
   The burden of your strife.
I am your staff of comfort,
   I will shield and protect you
Through life's complexities—
   Together we'll journey through.
I am the anchor of your soul,
   A safe place to run and hide,
I will never forsake you…
   I am always at your side.
I'm the lamp unto your way,
   With my Word I will guide.
I am the One whom you feel

---

1. Deborah Ann Belka, "Love Letter from God" used by permission from Deborah Ann Belka of Faith Writers, 2014, http://www.faithwriters.com. www.hiswingsshadow.com;http://poetrybydeborahann.wordpress.com/. See also "Father's Love Letter" in the conclusion to this book.

Stirring up deep inside.
I am your Creator,
    I knew you from the start;
That is why I gave to you
    For Me— a loving heart!

Now, create your own love letter to God—or "Dad." Get a pen and paper for everybody, and enjoy a few quiet moment together writing to God your love for Him, your hopes for His kingdom, and your plans to serve Him more purposefully in life, caring for His needs and His heart. Don't forget to thank God for being your heavenly Father and for loving you no matter what!

Prayer Community Activity

Have you ever considered inviting people to your home for a prayer meeting? Extend the praise/thanksgiving/confession/petitioning/closing prayer meeting format into your community group setting. Determine a meeting date, time, and location for a special prayer time with your group. Invite Christians who are interested in praying together, and explain to each guest that this will be a time of dedicated prayer in which families can pray aloud or silently. This is a wonderful way to become more open about your prayer life and to see answers to prayer flourish all around you. Ask each guest or family to come prepared with the following: 1) family name; 2) personal/family prayer concerns; 3) congregational prayer concerns; 4) kingdom hopes/prayers for God's glory to be magnified; and 5) a favorite Scripture.

Seat chairs in a circle and set the mood with some praise music playing in the background as people enter the room. Begin by forming a circle and going around the room with a simple praise and thanksgiving. If members do not wish to speak openly, they are certainly not required to. They can just sit, listen, and pray quietly if they wish.

Next, enter into a period of general confession, as is appropriate for a larger group. Then go around the circle asking everyone to refer to their prayer requests/information. Ask for prayer concerns by family. Once everyone has shared their prayer needs, lift concerns before the Lord as members feel led. Follow with congregational prayer concerns and kingdom prayers. Once all prayers are lifted, ask members to share their favorite Scripture and what it means to their family.

Conclude with a prayer and thank participants for joining in.

(Other Prayer Community Activities will refer to your "community group" or "small group." If you don't have a prayer group already, my hope is that as you gain comfortability and initiative, you will form a group of people who come together in prayer!)

DEVOTIONAL 2:
PRAYING FOR OUR FRIENDS

Family Minute

Dear God, help us understand why You want us to pray together and to pray for others. Help us to see that as two or more are gathered in Your holy name, You are in the midst. Amen.

[Peter] *went to the house of Mary, the mother of John whose other name was Mark, where many were gathered together and were praying.* (Acts 12:12)

True Story from Teresa's friend, Vergil Phillips

At church, I volunteered to be the "Large Group Story-Teller" for the kindergarten-through-second-grade kids. Most weeks, a generous number of kids would show up, all energized by sugar and pizza and ready for anything. We always began with singing and bouncing around, offering our thanks to the Lord and raising our heart rates enough to wear us out so that we could sit still for about twenty minutes and learn a story from the Bible.

We had settled in for the story when I noticed one of the second grade boys had tears in his eyes and a photo in his hand. "John?" I asked. "I see you're holding a picture of someone special. May I ask who it is?"

"It's my little cousin," he said, trying to manage a smile. "She has a brain tumor and will probably die soon. Doctors say they can't operate on her."

That hit me like a ton of bricks. Now *I* was the one choking back tears, in front of the whole room filled with children and adults, wearing my microphone, with all the stage lights on me. "Well, you know what I think we should do?" I responded. "I think we should pray!" And pray we did! We prayed directly to God, asking sincerely for this precious one to be healed. Nothing fancy, but we prayed with the innocence of children, and with a child's confident expectation of positive results.

A few weeks passed, and I decided, with some apprehension, to follow up with John. So I asked, "John, how's your little cousin?"

"Oh, she's fine!" he said matter-of-factly. "The tumor is gone."

A simple answer to prayer, just as we had expected—or should have expected. None of the children were surprised. They made a request to the almighty God, as we have taught them all along, and He can be trusted. Praise God! Of course He answered their prayers! And why wouldn't He answer them with a resounding *yes?* It dawned on me just then, there is great power in the prayers of the innocent to the almighty God. He is their God, and they are His children. Never underestimate the power of prayer, for our friends or for ourselves.[2]

2. Vergil Phillips is a member of the board of Child Family & Prison Ministry (CF&PM), Thailand. He and his wife, Christy, with their and adoptive daughter Stephanie continue to actively serve in church ministry.

Questions and Thoughts

1. Do you have a special friend who makes your day brighter?

It's important to remember our network of special friends in times of prayer. God encourages us to join together and seek Him on behalf of others. When we think of enjoyable family times, often our memories include these special people, don't they? It's good to remember our brothers and sisters in Christ as we pray.

2. Do you have certain friends you go to for prayer—like Peter did when he went to Mary's house?

It felt natural for Peter to go to them, to ask for agreement in prayer. As friends gathered around Peter in search of God's answers, it was an honor to connect with him to petition the Father.

3. Do you notice people who are sad or lonely and want to help? Do you have a friend in need of prayer?

Sometimes we need a shoulder to lean on when we are sad or need cheering-up. This instinct is a reflection of God's call to fellowship with one another.

Simple Prayers

For a particular friend:

Dear God in Heaven,
Praise Your holy name! Thank You for all of the wonderful friends we have, Lord. We especially want to thank You for _____. He/she has been a good friend, and we want to be a good friend in return. We ask You, Lord, to bless _____ and to help him/her to know how important they are. Thank You, Jesus! Amen.

For all friends:

Dear Heavenly Father,
Thank You, God, for our friends we hold close to our hearts. Thank You for the blessing they are to us. We pray, Lord, that we will always be here for each other. Help us, Lord, to be kind and to

love one another as You love us. Allow us to be supportive when our friends need it most. Thank You, Holy God! Amen.

For a friend in trouble:

Dear Father, we come before You today, powerful God, for Your mighty help and protection over our friend, _____. He/she needs You right now, and we ask You to rescue them in Your own amazing way. Thank You for giving us hearts that love. Help us to show more love to our friend and to remind them that they are not alone. Thank You, Lord, for hearing our prayer. In Jesus' name, we trust. Amen!

Scriptures about Friends

(Read through together; consider memorizing one.)

A friend loves at all times.   (Proverbs 17:17)

Love...your neighbor as yourself.   (Luke 10:27)

This is my commandment, that you love one another as I have loved you. Greater love has no one than this, that someone lay down his life for his friends.   (John 15:12–13)

Little children, let us not love in word or talk but in deed and in truth.   (1 John 3:18)

So whatever you wish that others would do to you, do also to them.   (Matthew 7:12)

God's Promises for Friends

A good man obtains favor from the LORD.   (Proverbs 12:2)

Again I say to you, if two of you agree on earth about anything they ask, it will be done for them by my Father in heaven.
                    (Matthew 18:19)

And let us not grow weary of doing good, for in due season we will reap, if we do not give up.   (Galatians 6:9)

Interactive Family Prayer

Option A: Prayer Jar

First, find a big jar and ask the kids if they would like to decorate the jar in any way. Put the jar in a special community place in your home with blank slips of paper and a pen or pencil next to it. Let everyone know that this is a jar for placing the names of friends or people to pray about anytime night or day.

Then, have family members take out the slips of paper at a certain time each week. Praise God for those individuals whose names are in the jar and pray for God's blessings over them. This can be a fun way to celebrate friendship, including friendships between siblings and parents.

Our family prays about each request until we feel the prayer has been answered or the situation is resolved. Sometimes, it takes a while to receive answers. When answers are delivered, we celebrate by praising God, thanking Him, and removing the request in God's glory.

Option B: A Simple Blessing

Center your child in the middle of the living room. Make them feel special—because they are surely special in the eyes of the Lord! Hold hands and touch the child you wish to pray over. Say a simple, special prayer concerning the child, and release thanksgiving to God for the amazing treasure they are in your lives.

Option C: Burning Bowl Prayers

Write down things you want to change in your life or to get rid of entirely—especially things that are getting in the way of your friendships with others or God. They can be pains, hurts, grudges, bad thoughts, bad memories, or bad habits. Explain to the family that it's important to make decisions to let go of these things. As Paul said in the Bible, *"Do not conform to the pattern of this world, but be transformed by the renewing of your mind"* (Romans 12:2 NIV). Then, place the slips of paper in a steel bowl (or other fireproof container) one by one as a family. Venture outside together and have an adult to burn the slips of paper. As you watch the papers shrivel in flames, release the bad and be prepared for the good to come. It's a fun way to let go of the past. It's also a technique to free people from their troubles and insecurities. Just remember, the old must go and the new is on its way. Pray that you would trust God to help you be free of old burdens and to welcome His blessings anew.

Prayer Community Activity

Hold a special prayer time with guests to offer short one-sentence prayers called "Popcorn Prayers" for friends you care about and also for those in need. Popcorn prayers don't typically include a beginning or end; instead, one person starts, and everyone just says a sentence out loud, whether of petition, praise, or thanksgiving. We've found that popcorn prayers are especially entertaining for children!

You could….

+ Before inviting people over for popcorn prayers, ask a local convalescent center for a list of widows or elders who could use some prayer and companionship. Then, during the popcorn prayer, pray for the people whose names you received and encourage group members to visit them!

+ Offer popcorn as a snack. Pop some bags of popcorn and have group members bring the toppings such as cheese, extra butter, garlic salt, bacon seasoning, chocolate chips for melting, cinnamon/sugar, etc.

+ Show a video about a child foster care or adoption program and how members can help.

+ Show a video from a local animal shelter of pets available for adoption.

+ Play "Guess the Kernels." Have a large jar of kernels present and ask members to guess how many kernels fill the jar. Winner earns movie passes or a movie family fun kit.

+ If the meeting is close to a holiday, guests could stay after the prayer time to string popcorn for Halloween or Christmas decorations.

DEVOTIONAL 3:
PRAYING FOR OUR SALVATION AND OUR CHURCH

Family Minute

Dear God, help us to be prepared for Your powerful return. Let us be ready for Your incredible presence. Let Your almighty glory be shown to all the world. May many more accept You as Savior now. Thank You, Jesus! Amen.

For it is written, "As I live, says the Lord, every knee shall bow to me, and every tongue shall confess to God."

(Romans 14:11)

True Story from Teresa

One of our favorite family worship songs is Mercy Me's "I Can Only Imagine." We listen to its lyrics and envision falling to our knees at the sight of our Lord and Savior. Maybe you have heard this song, or wondered what it will be like to finally see Jesus!

Several years ago, I had a dream Jesus was coming…but I wasn't ready. I saw flashes of lightning, heard the roar of thunder, and witnessed people scattering in fear and chaos in the streets. Fire and destruction broke out all around us. In a flash, I woke up feeling a sense of shock and frustration.

In my startled state, I knew it was time to commit my life wholeheartedly to God. I had to talk with a pastor and share this dream. I asked Jesus for forgiveness and agreed to be baptized. As I walked into the baptismal, I giggled inside because the pastor wore waders and rubber boots. He actually got into the water with me. *Now, this is the way to be baptized,* I thought.

During the precious moments in the water with my family gathered all around me, I recalled when I first gave my heart to Jesus at a young age. It was the joy of my life knowing I was safe in Jesus' arms. I was thankful for the guidance of a pastor, and knew that my church family would continue to stand alongside of me.

Questions and Thoughts

1. If you saw Jesus today, what would you do? Would you jump up and run quickly to be with Him? What would you say to Jesus?

Maybe you would present Him with a special prayer request or ask Him to fill your heart with peace and love. Some may plead with God to help them practice family hope and forgiveness.

2. If Jesus comes back in the clouds today, are you ready to meet Him? Have you given your heart completely to Jesus?

+ If no, then maybe this is the time. Pray to the Lord this simple prayer with the words of your own heart:

Lord Jesus, I ask You into my heart. I'm a sinner so please forgive my sins and save me. I believe You died on the cross for my sins. Thank You for all You did for me to offer me eternal life. Thank

You for hearing my prayers and for loving me no matter what. Please help me to walk closer with You each day. Thank You, Jesus. It's in Your holy name I pray. Amen.

✦ If yes, have you made the Lord your Guide and priority? Do you spend enough time with Him each day?

Prayer, worship, and baptism offer hope and refreshment for the human spirit. Peace replaces pandemonium in our lives when we spend more time with Jesus. God knows our hearts whether we are walking with Him, fully on board with His teachings, or slowly walking away. Every day spent in relationship with Jesus draws us closer to His heavenly kingdom.

3. How can going to church help us walk more closely with Jesus? How can we help others walk more closely with Jesus?

A Simple Prayer for the Church

Dear Loving Father,

We thank You today for our church and that we are followers of Jesus Christ. Please keep us faithful in service to You, Holy God. Bless our church with ability, passion, and opportunity to reach the lost who need to hear Your message. Let it all be to Your glory. In Jesus' name, we pray. Amen.

A Simple Prayer for Our Pastor/ Priest

Thank You, Lord, for the light of Your message. Thank You that You have given Pastor _____ the good news to preach to Your people. We pray that You will be with him/her each and every day and speak through him/her Your message to the lost, hungry, and hurting. Help Pastor _____ to be a servant of Your purpose, bringing many closer to Your salvation. Let it all be for Your glory.

Thank You, Jesus. Amen!

Scriptures About Our Sure Salvation

(Read through together; consider memorizing one.)

For I am not ashamed of the gospel, for it is the power of God for salvation to everyone who believes.   (Romans 1:16)

Whoever confesses that Jesus is the Son of God, God abides in him, and he in God.   (1 John 4:15)

If we confess our sins, he is faithful and just to forgive us our sins and to cleanse us from all unrighteousness.   (1 John 1:9)

Scriptures for Our Church and Spiritual Leaders

Arise, shine, for your light has come, and the glory of the LORD has risen upon you.   (Isaiah 60:1)

And day by day, attending the temple together and breaking bread in their homes, they received their food with glad and generous hearts, praising God and having favor with all the people. And the Lord added to their number day by day those who were being saved.   (Acts 2:46–47)

Obey your leaders and submit to them, for they are keeping watch over your souls, as those who will have to give an account. Let them do this with joy and not with groaning, for that would be of no advantage to you.   (Hebrews 13:17)

God's Promises for the Church

So shall my word be that goes out from my mouth; it shall not return to me empty, but it shall accomplish that which I purpose, and shall succeed in the thing for which I sent it.

(Isaiah 55:11)

And we know that for those who love God all things work together for good, for those who are called according to his purpose.   (Romans 8:28)

I am the light of the world. Whoever follows me will not walk in darkness, but will have the light of life.   (John 8:12)

"I promised that your house and the house of your father should go in and out before me forever," but now the Lord declares: "Far be it from me, for those who honor me I will honor, and those who despise me shall be lightly esteemed."
                                    (1 Samuel 2:30)

Interactive Family Prayer

Option A: The Importance of Tithing

This activity focuses on Malachi 3:10–11 as one of the primary passages of the Bible that explains why tithing (giving a part of our income) is so important to God. It's important to teach this passage to our family, not only so that our church may be blessed by the firstfruits of our income, but also to bring glory to God and ensure blessings and favor.

Sit down as a family and read Malachi 3:10–11, then move through the questions and answers:

Bring the full tithe into the storehouse, that there may be food in my house. And thereby put me to the test, says the Lord of hosts, if I will not open the windows of heaven for you and pour down for you a blessing until there is no more need. I will rebuke the devourer for you, so that it will not destroy the fruits of your soil, and your vine in the field shall not fail to bear, says the Lord of hosts.

1. What does it mean to *"bring the full tithe into the storehouse, that there may be food in my house"?*

This means that you and your family must bring a portion of your income earned first *to God.*

2. Does that seem like too much?

Remember that we do it in order to be blessed! God says, "Put me to the test…if I will not open the windows of heaven for you and pour down a blessing until there is no more need." This is one of the only sections in the Bible where God says, "Put me to the test," or in other words, "try it out!" We as a family should bring our tithes to the church for His sake and because He commands us, and when we do this, He will pour out a blessing and fulfill our family needs.

3. Does our attitude about giving matter?

Yes—our attitude matters. The apostle Paul tells us exactly how to give! "The point is this: whoever sows sparingly will also reap sparingly, and whoever sows bountifully will also reap bountifully. Each one must give as he has decided in his heart, not reluctantly or under compulsion, for God loves a cheerful giver" (2 Corinthians 9:6–8). Wow, it doesn't get much plainer than that. Our lives will be full of chances and opportunities to give— whether of money, time, or resources. May we always endeavor to give cheerfully!

Show your child a physical example—from your bank statement or from a sheet of paper with a sum gross total of income—of taking out the ten percent and writing a check to your church or making a deposit into your family church home. If you don't have a church home, consider gifting the tithe to a local church you visit or to a ministry of your choice. Then, read again as a family the Malachi 3:10–11 blessing to you and yours.[3]

---

3. For further reference on where "ten percent" comes from in the Bible and other complexities of tithing, see the helpful message, "Toward the Tithe and Beyond: How God Funds His Work," http://www.desiringgod.org/messages/toward-the-tithe-and-beyond (accessed April 8, 2016).

Option B: Volunteers On Board

Call your church and ask for a one- to two-hour volunteer project where you can assist for a short period of time in the evening. As you serve as God calls you, take moments to pray about the church activities going on that evening. This is a modest method of teaching children how important it is to give away our time to God and others.

Option C: Make Loaves of Bread to Share

Follow the recipe below to make a quick bread mix to share with friends, church members, or neighbors in God's love. Place in clear bags, tie with a ribbon, and attach a prayer for the recipient(s). If you are not a baker, buy a fresh-baked loaf of bread and attach the Scripture with a bow.

Quick Bread Recipe (makes 4 loaves)

Baking mix: 12 cups all-purpose flour
6 cups white sugar
12 tsp. baking powder
6 tsp. baking soda
6 tsp. salt

Wet ingredients: ½ cup vegetable oil
2 eggs

Instructions: Mix flour, sugar, baking powder, soda, and salt thoroughly. (Can be stored on the shelf for months.) Mix 3 cups baking mix, oil, and eggs. Add 1 cup of mixed nuts, raisins, or dates, etc., if desired. Pour into one 8.5 x 4.5 or two 7.5 x 3.5 greased loaf pans. Bake at 350° F for 30 to 45 minutes.

Add a Scripture message to each loaf of bread such as: "*Blessed is the man who trusts in the LORD, whose trust is the LORD*" (Jeremiah 17:7).

Prayer Community Activity

Host a night of testimony! I began this devotional with a short version of my testimony. Have you ever noticed how important testimonies are in the Bible? The psalmist often exclaims that he will talk about the greatness of the Lord in the midst of the congregation—or in other words, in front of other believers! (See, for example, Psalm 22:22–24; 71:14–24.) Similarly, in the New Testament, there are numerous examples of men and women speaking and testifying about what Jesus has done for them. (See, for example, John 4:28–30; 9:8–25; Acts 4:13–22; 22:1–21.) God uses our testimonies for His glory!

With this in mind, host a night of testimony for believers and their families. Remember that it can be so amazing for children to hear the story of how their parents came to faith if they've never heard it before! Ask whoever is comfortable to briefly share their testimony—that is, how God brought them to Himself and how He has changed their lives. Close the evening with a time of thanking God for being mighty enough to change our hearts and so loving that He continues to mold us and shape us into useful vessels for Him!

DEVOTIONAL 4:

PRAYING FOR STUDENTS, SCHOOLS, AND TEACHERS

Family Minute

God, help us to be one with You and to share in fellowship and hope for others. May the world be a brighter place because of our purpose for You. Thank You, Jesus! It's in Your holy name, we pray. Amen.

Love one another as I have loved you. (John 15:12)

True Story from Teresa

Mrs. McClelland is the teacher I remember most from childhood. Young, smart, and beautiful, she loved every child in the class and encouraged us at every step. She taught us the joy of learning. She prompted us to be ourselves and to remain strong in our convictions. Once, she organized a field trip to the Missouri state capitol for the entire fourth grade class. I know it must have taken a great deal of planning and effort. On this way-above-average outing for fourth graders, I remember standing on the capitol steps believing in the possibility of a bright, astonishing future for me and the rest of my class.

At the end of the year, Mrs. McClelland left the school to start a family. I missed her terribly. I guess she thought of us, too, because she invited some of the girls to her home for a brunch. This was the first brunch I ever attended, and I felt very grown-up and important. It is one of my most cherished memories.

Years later, I attended a special service at church and to my incredible surprise, there Mrs. McClelland sat, right behind me. We hugged and exchanged recollections of our time together. We rejoiced to see each other again. I left church that night with a smile that could not be wiped away.

Questions and Thoughts

1. Do you have a favorite school, homeschool co-op, church, or classroom teacher who has blessed your life?

2. Do you recall a time when you were cheered by someone special who made you feel like you really mattered—and that you would do great things in life?

Teachers and mentors help us to uncover the joy of learning and sometimes they inspire us to seek our dreams. Part of the process involves revealing our inner identity. Who are we? Who made us? What are we meant to do on this planet? How can we make a real, profound difference?

3. Are you a teacher in anybody's life?

Thinking of these important influences from our past or present can remind us of God's greatest commandment to "love one another as I have loved you." As these teachers have loved us, we should love them and others with the same love. Go, therefore, and encourage others to seek Jesus. If you have younger siblings, don't forget that they look up to you, in a way, as a "teacher." Let us also cheer on those teachers, leaders, and mentors in our lives who truly make a difference for Christ, impacting those around them.

A Simple Prayer for Students

Dear God,

Thank You for giving me the spirit of learning. We thank You for the mind, an amazing creation of Your holy power. Help me to be the best student I can be, to learn all You want me to learn, and to be obedient and kind to my teachers. Please grant me the wisdom to share Your Word whenever I can with my fellow students. Help me to be focused on Your will and Your purpose, so that I reach the goals ahead of me to Your glory.

Thank You, God, for my school, my teachers, and for all that I am able to learn this year. Please bless my school with Your great and powerful protection. Please place Your holy hand over this wonderful place and make sure that no evil comes near it. We trust that Your angels will guard us, keeping it a safe place to learn.

We pray that all the teachers, principals, coaches, and counselors would walk in Your way and be instructors in Your goodness. Thank You for watching over everyone at my school. In Jesus' name, I pray. Amen!

Scriptures for Students

(Read through together; consider memorizing one.)

The steps of a man are established by the LORD, when he delights in his way.   (Psalm 37:23)

Remember also your Creator in the days of your youth, before the evil days come.   (Ecclesiastes 12:1)

You guide me with your counsel, and afterward you will receive me to glory. (Psalm 73:24)

In all your ways acknowledge him, and he will make straight your paths. (Proverbs 3:6)

Apply your heart to instruction and your ear to words of knowledge. (Proverbs 23:12)

God's Promises for Students

Truly, truly, I say to you, whoever believes in me will also do the works that I do; and greater works than these will he do, because I am going to the Father. (John 14:12)

The reward for humility and fear of the LORD *is riches and honor and life.* (Proverbs 22:4)

Prize [wisdom] highly, and she will exalt you; she will honor you if you embrace her. (Proverbs 4:8)

The memory of the righteous is a blessing. (Proverbs 10:7)

Simple Prayer for Teachers

Dear Father,

You are the Creator of all things including our teachers in the community. We thank You for magnificent leaders who care about our education. We pray for a successful future. We ask You to bless all those in our school who teach and learn. We ask You to guide everyone in their abilities, to encourage them, and to help them to be more like You. Help them to be patient, kind, and understanding. Guide them in Your ways.

In Jesus' holy name, we pray. Amen!

Scriptures for Teachers

And what great nation is there, that has statutes and rules so righteous as all this law that I set before you today?
(Deuteronomy 4:8)

You shall teach them diligently to your children.
(Deuteronomy 6:7)

Train up a child in the way he should go; even when he is old he will not depart from it.   (Proverbs 22:6)

All your children shall be taught by the LORD, and great shall be the peace of your children.   (Isaiah 54:13)

And you shall warn them about the statutes and the laws, and make them know the way in which they must walk and what they must do.   (Exodus 18:20)

God's Promises Concerning Teachers

Ask, and you will receive, that your joy may be full.
(John 16:24)

And whatever you ask in prayer, you will receive, if you have faith.   (Matthew 21:22)

Call to me and I will answer you, and will tell you great and hidden things that you have not known.   (Jeremiah 33:3)

If you ask me anything in my name, I will do it.   (John 14:14)

Interactive Family Prayer

Option A: Alphabet Prayers

For each letter of the alphabet, think of a topic related to school, students, or teachers to pray about. Pray through the alphabet out loud. As each family member says a letter, someone should blurt out the first school-related thing that comes to mind beginning with that letter and pray about that topic. For example: for A: academics—praying to be the best students possible; B: Box Tops—to collect the most Box Tops for your classroom; C: caring for teachers, etc. List something for every letter. If you can't think of something, just move to the next letter.

Option B: Prayer Journaling

Provide every family member with a prayer journal. The purpose of this journal is to encourage each family member—big or small—to record his or her thoughts, hopes, and prayers. If a child is too small, give them a journal anyway and remind them to let you know about anything that's on their mind. Then, you can write it down for them. You can also ask them to draw a picture of what they are thinking or praying about.

The journal offers individuals a special place to share their hearts and grow closer to God. They can carry this in their backpacks to and from school, church, and anywhere they wish.

Ask everyone to bring this prayer journal to your daily—or weekly—family prayer sessions. Ask individual family members if there are subjects on their hearts or recorded in their journal they would like to pray about. It may be related to their friends at school, a test they are concerned about, or thoughts about a teacher.

Spend a few moments praying over each person's prayer requests. Finish by thanking God offering gratitude for His great love over you. As a way to promote closeness to God, enable family members to purchase new journals each year or every quarter. Encourage them to keep their writings in a sacred place for future reflection.

Option C: Sporting Prayers

Pick your family's favorite sporting event. Attend the event and pray for God to achieve glory through the team's success—whether it's a win or loss, may He receive the honor and praise. You could have moments of Courtside Prayers, Fifty-Yard-Line Prayers, or even Soccer Field Prayers—whatever you do, let God be your guide in praying for the team and God's plan for them and your family.

Prayer Community Activity

Adopt and pray for a school! Talk with your family or group about a school that is in need because of recent issues or hardships, whether of violence, financial difficulty, negative press, staff retention difficulty, or others. Adopt this school as a family and send its administrators special notes, emails, and messages of encouragement. You can also learn more via websites like adoptaschool.org, everyschool.com/adopt_map, or join the National Adopt a School Initiative by going online to churchadoptaschool.org.

DEVOTIONAL 5:
PRAYING AT MEALTIMES

Family Minute

Dear God, we are thankful for Your great care over our needs. Thank You for food, water, and a place to call home. Please help us to remember those less fortunate. We sing Your praises in Jesus' name. Amen.

It is good to give thanks to the LORD, to sing praises to your name, O Most High. (Psalm 92:1)

True Story from Teresa

One of our favorite things to do as a family is to eat together. Sometimes, like many Americans, we overdo it with our focus on food and snacks. However, our perspective changed a number of years ago when we traveled to Kazakhstan to adopt our son. While there, we repeatedly saw homeless people digging in the trash for their meals.

What a devastating sight for a family who enjoys food! It made us acutely aware that not everyone is blessed like many of us here in America. Not all families have the means to buy groceries, eat out at nice restaurants, or consume their fill of food three or more times a day.

In fact, many children throughout the world, including in our own country, go hungry each night. Some consider themselves fortunate to receive just one meal a day. How we would grumble if we had to go without a single meal! Yet, thankfully, we don't suffer in such a way.

Questions and Thoughts

1. Have you ever been around the homeless?

2. Have you seen their suffering firsthand?

3. Have you ever felt their pain within in your heart?

4. Have you ever gone without a meal and felt that hunger pain in the pit of your stomach? What if you had to go all day without any food to eat?

If you are thankful for God's provisions and abundant blessings, join in a prayer of gratitude.

A Simple Prayer of Mealtime Thanks

Dear Loving Father,

Thank You for being a great Provider. Thank You for all You have given us. Thank You for Your Son, our Savior. Thank You for our family. Thank You for Your light and love, and this food we are about to eat. For all of these things, we give thanks. Please give Your daily bread to all those in need. Please forgive us our sins and help us to live in joy with You forevermore. In Jesus' holy name, we pray. Amen.

A Simple Cafeteria Prayer

Dear God,

Bless this food before me today. Help it to nourish my body. Thank You for all that I have. It's in Your heavenly name I pray. Amen.

A Simple Prayer of Thanksgiving

Thank You, Lord, for Your holy presence in our lives. Thank You for all that You have given us. Thank You for Your love that is amazing and true. Thank You for this food, which is more than we could have asked for. In Jesus' precious name, we pray and give thanks. Amen.

Scriptures of Thanksgiving

(Read through together; consider memorizing one.)

So, whether you eat or drink, or whatever you do, do all to the glory of God.   (1 Corinthians 10:31)

Also that everyone should eat and drink and take pleasure in all his toil—this is God's gift to man.   (Ecclesiastes 3:13)

You shall eat the fruit of the labor of your hands; you shall be blessed, and it shall be well with you.   (Psalm 128:2)

Enter his gates with thanksgiving, and his courts with praise! Give thanks to him; bless his name!   (Psalm 100:4)

I will give thanks to the LORD with my whole heart; I will recount all of your wonderful deeds.   (Psalm 9:1)

The one who offers thanksgiving as his sacrifice glorifies me; to one who orders his way rightly I will show the salvation of God!   (Psalm 50:23)

Do not be anxious about anything, but in everything by prayer and supplication with thanksgiving let your requests be made known to God. (Philippians 4:6)

God's Promises for Our Welfare

The righteous has enough to satisfy his appetite. (Proverbs 13:25)

You shall eat in plenty and be satisfied, and praise the name of the LORD *your God.* (Joel 2:26)

I will abundantly bless her provisions; I will satisfy her poor with bread. (Psalm 132:15)

He makes peace in your borders; he fills you with the finest of the wheat. (Psalm 147:14)

Interactive Family Prayer

Option A: Prayer Dinner

Ask each family member to bring a prayer for the homeless, orphans, widows, or less fortunate to the table. Go around before and after dinner and pray about those who suffer in our world and pray about specific measures your family can take to help in the future. Is there a local soup kitchen to volunteer at? A food pantry to volunteer for? Recite as a family James 1:27: *"Religion that God our Father accepts as pure and faultless is this: to look after orphans and widows in their distress and to keep oneself from being polluted by the world"* (NIV).

Option B: Top Ten Thankfulness List

Ask each family member to write a list of the top ten things they are thankful for and compare the lists. Items included could be family, friends, good food, nice weather, an income, or a favorite place or activity. If a child is too young to write, parents can ask them to say the things they are thankful for and record them on a piece of paper. Ask them to bring the lists to dinner. From there, create one master list of common thanks. Then, pray a prayer of thanksgiving together to God for all blessings He has given your family. Post the master list in a highly visible place, like the refrigerator or taped to a kitchen cupboard so that everyone can be reminded of it regularly!

Prayer Community Activity

Ask over a few friends, family members, or neighbors to join you for a potluck and to bring a dish or a side to share. Maybe even include a menu that looks like this:

Salad: Praise [praise God for His goodness!]

Main Dish: Thanksgiving [Give thanks, including a Scripture of thanks]

Side: Confession [Releasing all burdens to God]

Dessert: Petitioning [Pray over one another's needs]

Coffee/Drinks: Closing prayer of thanks

In preparation, ask your children to make placemats for each guest out of large pieces of construction paper and decorate with a Scripture from this chapter and with the "menu" above.

Then, join together with friends and family once they've arrived. Hold hands and say a blessing over the group. Share in a meal and a conversation about God and His great care. Then, hold a prayer session following the format above.

DEVOTIONAL 6:

PRAYING FOR OUR SAFETY, SLEEP, AND SECURITY

Family Minute

Thank You, God! You are our Rock and our salvation. You strengthen us when we seek You. Help us to seek You, heavenly Father, more and more. Bless this time together as a family. It's in Jesus' powerful name, we pray. Amen!

Fear not, for I am with you; be not dismayed, for I am your God; I will strengthen you, I will help you, I will uphold you with my righteous right hand. (Isaiah 41:10)

True Story from Teresa

One day, I was making my kids' sack lunches for school the next day and realized that we had run out of sandwich bags and chips. As the mom, I did what moms do and jumped in the car to run errands. After I picked up what I needed, I headed home. But when I pulled out of the grocery store's parking lot, a car came barreling out of nowhere and struck me nearly head on. My car spun completely around and crashed into a side railing. I blacked out instantly.

I recall waking up to smoke pouring from the engine and wreckage hemming me in. An ambulance, a firetruck, and emergency vehicles all had sirens screaming, and police swarmed around me. The other car appeared to be totaled.

My first thought was *oh no, this is a tragedy! Why me?* But as I gained consciousness, I realized that not a single scratch showed on either me or the driver of the car that hit me. Both vehicles were entirely demolished from a maximum-impact crash, and we should have both been taken from the scene by ambulance and rushed to a hospital. Instead, we walked away unharmed. That is a purely God's grace.

The amazing part of this story, as I reflect, is that we always pray as a family for safety and protection. Thanks be to Jesus for His safety and security even when we don't see it firsthand. Praise Him for His supernatural ability to guard and protect us.

Questions and Thoughts

1. Have you ever been in an accident, or do you know someone who has experienced a major collision or disaster?

We all face troubles at various points of our lives. Sometimes, we just need God's hand of protection to secure us.

2. Have you or a family member ever faced safety or security risks or concerns?

Maybe you know somebody who has been in the face of terror, fire, theft, or welfare concerns.

3. Have you ever been scared about something and wondered how you would make it through?

God is our almighty Defender. Yes, fears can halt us from living a successful life if we allow them. Yet, God has all of the power to release our worries if only we seek Him first in prayer. Remember that Isaiah 41:10 tells us to "Fear not, for I am with you, be not dismayed, for I am your God; I will strengthen you, I will help you, I will uphold you with my righteous right hand." *Remember, God is here and ready to uphold us with His righteous right hand!*

Simple Prayer for Safety

Dear Lord,

Thank You for the safety and protection You give to my family and friends each day. I pray You will continue to hold us close in Your sight. Keep us free from evil or troubles. I pray that everywhere we go, You will be with us. I pray for the power of Your protection always. In Jesus' name, I trust. Amen.

Prayer for Good Sleep/Rest

Dear Heavenly Father,

Thank You for being my Father who watches over me at night. As I lay down to sleep, I ask for Your heavenly peace over my body, mind, and spirit. I pray for quiet rest throughout the night. I pray that when I awake, I will be all ready for a new day. In Jesus' mighty name, I pray. Amen.

A Prayer for Safe Travel

Dear Heavenly Father,

Today, we leave on a trip, and we reach out asking You to be with us on our journey. We ask You, dear Lord, to bless our trip with Your complete safety. We pray for no troubles or delays. We pray that Your almighty hand will protect us wherever we are and whatever we do, in Jesus' holy name. Thank You, Lord! Amen.

Scriptures on Safety, Sleep, and Security

(Read through together; consider memorizing one.)

The beloved of the LORD dwells in safety. The High God surrounds him all day long, and dwells between his shoulders.
(Deuteronomy 33:12)

The name of the LORD is a strong tower; the righteous man runs into it and is safe.   (Proverbs 18:10)

I have set the LORD always before me; because he is at my right hand, I shall not be shaken.   (Psalm 16:8)

He is not afraid of bad news; his heart is firm, trusting in the LORD.   (Psalm 112:7)

And you will feel secure, because there is hope; you will look around and take your rest in security.   (Job 11:18)

I lift up my eyes to the hills. From where does my help come? My help comes from the LORD, who made heaven and earth.
(Psalm 121:1–2)

I will make you lie down in safety.   (Hosea 2:18)

In peace I will both lie down and sleep; for you alone, O LORD, make me dwell in safety.   (Psalm 4:8)

If you lie down, you will not be afraid; when you lie down, your sleep will be sweet.   (Proverbs 3:24)

The peace of God, which surpasses all understanding, will guard your hearts and your minds in Christ Jesus.
(Philippians 4:7)

Come to me, all who labor and are heavy laden, and I will give you rest.   (Matthew 11:28)

God's Promises for Our Safety and Rest

In the fear of the LORD *one has strong confidence, and his children will have a refuge.*   (Proverbs 14:26)

The house of the righteous will stand.   (Proverbs 12:7)

You will walk on your way securely, and your foot will not stumble.   (Proverbs 3:23)

Whoever listens to me will dwell secure and will be at ease, without dread of disaster.   (Proverbs 1:33)

Interactive Family Prayer

Option A: Fire-Flight Activity

Recite Psalm 91 to put out the fires of the enemy.

Those who live in the shelter of the Most High
will find rest in the shadow of the Almighty.
This I declare about the LORD:
He alone is my refuge, my place of safety;
He is my God, and I trust him.
For he will rescue you from every trap
and protect you from deadly disease.
He will cover you with his feathers.
He will shelter you with his wings.
His faithful promises are your armor and protection.
Do not be afraid of the terrors of the night,
nor the arrow that flies in the day.
Do not dread the disease that stalks in darkness,
nor the disaster that strikes at midday.

Though a thousand fall at your side,
though ten thousand are dying around you,
these evils will not touch you.

> *Just open your eyes,*
> *and see how the wicked are punished.*
>
> *If you make the* LORD *your refuge,*
> *if you make the Most High your shelter,*
> *no evil will conquer you;*
> *no plague will come near your home.*
> *For he will order his angels*
> *to protect you wherever you go.*
> *They will hold you up with their hands*
> *so you won't even hurt your foot on a stone.*
> *You will trample upon lions and cobras;*
> *you will crush fierce lions and serpents under your feet!*
>
> *The* LORD *says, "I will rescue those who love me.*
> *I will protect those who trust in my name.*
> *When they call on me, I will answer;*
> *I will be with them in trouble.*
> *I will rescue and honor them.*
> *I will reward them with a long life*
> *and give them my salvation."*

(Psalm 91 NLT)

Pray for safety, security and rest for each family member according to this Scripture. Psalm 91 promises that God will be our refuge and protection in all situations as long as we seek Him. So, seek Him together as a family and learn about this powerful Word of God. For Ephesians 6:17 says, "[Take] *the helmet of salvation, and the sword of the Spirit, which is the word of God.*" The Word of God is our weapon against the enemy—the devil's attacks.

Option B: Family Emergency Planning

Develop a family plan for fires, weather, and other emergencies. Discuss a safe place your family can go to nearby if you are ever separated. Then, pray for God to bless your plan.

Option C: Home Blessing Ceremony

Walk through your house as a family, stop in each room, and pray. In the child's bedroom, pray for their rest and safety. In the parents' work areas, pray for peace. In the kitchen, pray for health, strength, and fellowship. In the dining room, pray for good conversations. In the home office—if you have one—pray for financial success, and in the garage, pray for the safe running of your vehicles. Ask your children for other ideas of what to pray for in each room! Then, pray over your children, and ask God to bless them at home, in their lives, and in the future.

Prayer Community Activity

As a community group, form a service prayer committee. Adopt a local fire or police department to pray for each week. Ask the fire marshal or police chief to join your group to give an overview about their unit and its specific needs and challenges. They may not be Christians, but may still appreciate the attention and concern! Pray about these requests each week. Write prayer notes to individual fire- and police- men and women, asking for God's protection and safety over them. Visit the local police or fire department together. Ask your kids to draw pictures to take to the fire- and police- men and women. Alternatively, invite the whole crew to your group for a special potluck or dessert time, offering moments of prayer and thanksgiving for their service and God's favor over them.

DEVOTIONAL 7:
PRAYING FOR OUR WORLD, NATION, AND COMMUNITY

Family Minute

Dear God, please have mercy on our nation and community. Please allow us Your peace and keep us free of harm. We realize You are our safe haven in storms and troubles. Thank You for being our Rescuer, in Jesus' mighty name, we pray. Amen.

Peace I leave with you; my peace I give to you. Not as the world gives do I give to you. Let not your hearts be troubled, neither let them be afraid. (John 14:27)

True Story from Teresa

Late in the afternoon of May 22, 2011, the deadliest tornado in the US in half a century struck Joplin, Missouri. With fierce winds of over 200 mph and a path a mile wide, the tornado ripped through streets, homes, parking lots, and businesses.

Before it arrived, our cousin Sarah (one of several relatives of ours who live in Joplin!) got in the car to pick up dinner and dog food. When she reached the center of town, sirens began going off, but she didn't realize what was happening and traveled on to Walmart. She parked and walked inside only to find the store manager shouting to her and other customers, "You can *not* shop right now. You have to either go to the back for shelter or leave immediately!" A voice inside her told her to leave, so Sarah got back into her Jeep and started to exit. She drove to the west side of the parking lot and felt a strong urge to park. So she did, and the rain stormed uncontrollably. She thought to herself, "I can still drive home in this." But just then a shopping cart hit the side of her vehicle, and the back hatch shattered. Sarah shared with our family, "I started to pray, 'God, You are with me' over and over. At one point I heard something inside me say 'Take your foot off the brake.'" Sarah did what God told her, and at that moment, her vehicle turned abruptly from facing west to facing north.

Even as Sarah was in the parking lot, the tornado had torn the metal roof off the Walmart building beside her and dropped parts of it on the customers and employees inside. A support beam fell on a family and instantly killed them. The total death count at the Walmart was 89; according to CNN, the tornado that struck Joplin killed 158 people and injured more than a thousand.[4] It was a devastating tragedy.

As we hear of such tornadoes, earthquakes, and tragedies around the world and in our own country, we are called to take action, pray, and *"bear one another's burdens"* (Galatians 6:2). The city of Joplin estimates that over 130,000 volunteers turned out after the storm and over the following year to help families rebuild. Praise God for His protection and His love shown through the actions of caring people. None of us would be here without the life-giving grace coverage of our almighty God!

---

4. "10 deadliest U. S. tornadoes on record," CNN.com, April 27, 2013, http://www.cnn.com/2013/01/30/us/deadliest-tornadoes/.

Questions and Thoughts

1. Have you ever been in a storm?

We hear of tornadoes, earthquakes, floods, and man-made tragedies around the world and in our own country.

2. When you see devastation as it fills the news, do you feel the pain of those suffering?

3. Has your town or community experienced a hardship or disaster?

4. Are you concerned for the world and our nation? For your future?

God has the power to protect us. He can save us from the storms of our lives. Let us seek Him together in prayer.

A Simple Prayer for World Peace

Dear God of Light and Truth,

We thank You for all of the people of our world and our nation. We thank You for caring for us. We pray for Your holy power to be with us, especially with our world leaders, to keep peace with other nations. We place our trust in Your powers to bring good to the world. We trust You will overcome evil. We pray for hope for those who are suffering. Help us to reach out and lend a hand to people in need. Please bring peace to all people, reminding us that You created us by Your powerful and holy hand. Thank You, God! Amen.

A Simple Prayer for Our Nation

Dear Almighty God,

Thank You for our wonderful nation and for all of the freedoms that You grant us. We ask that You to protect our county from war and disaster. We ask You to guide and direct our president and leaders in all of their decisions. Give them strength and courage to always do what is right and to act by Your will, Holy God, and never by self-serving agendas. Please protect our rights as free citizens and help our future to be bright and peaceful. In Jesus' powerful name we pray and trust. Amen.

A Simple Prayer for Our Community

Dear Powerful Father,

Thank You for this community that we love and enjoy. Thank You for each person You have brought to live here in our area. We pray for peace for our citizens, for good choices by those who are in authority, and for Your holy hand to rest over this community. We ask You to enable us to live in peace, showing respect for one another, always striving for what is good and acceptable in Your sight. In Jesus' holy name, we pray and trust. Amen.

Scriptures on Our World, Nation, and Community

(Read through together; consider memorizing one.)

For the earth shall be full of the knowledge of the LORD as the waters cover the sea. (Isaiah 11:9)

Blessed shall you be in the city, and blessed shall you be in the field. (Deuteronomy 28:3)

And the peace of God, which surpasses all understanding, will guard your hearts and your minds in Christ Jesus.
(Philippians 4:7)

O LORD, you will ordain peace for us, for you have indeed done for us all our works. (Isaiah 26:12)

He makes peace in your borders. (Psalm 147:14)

God's Promises for Our World

> I will give peace in the land, and you shall lie down, and none shall make you afraid. (Leviticus 26:6)

> May the LORD give strength to his people! May the LORD bless his people with peace! (Psalm 29:11)

> Peace be upon Israel. (Psalm 125:5)

> Great peace have those who love your law; nothing can make them stumble. (Psalm 119:165)

> My people will abide in a peaceful habitation, in secure dwellings, and in quiet resting places. (Isaiah 32:18)

Interactive Family Prayer

Option A: Attend a Community or Congregational Prayer Service

+ Remember the National Day of Prayer, which occurs annually the first Thursday in May. Many churches and cities do special services that are open to the public. Check online at www.nationaldayofprayer.org. It can be a great opportunity to join with your neighbors in prayer.

+ Remember the World Day of Prayer, which occurs annually the first Friday of March. Check for events in your area online at www.worlddayofprayer.net or via email at admin@worlddayofprayer.net.

+ Join a prayer chain, church prayer group, or reconnect with another prayer group in your life.

+ Form your own email or social media group prayer chain. All you have to do is email or call a few friends and ask for their participation. Track prayer needs and check back on a regular basis. You may even develop a shared Google drive where you can post prayer needs and add to prayer updates via Google docs. Set up an app via apps.google.com/products/drive/.

Option B: Pray for Those Who Serve Us

Call your neighborhood watch leader, police chief, mayor, politician, or other city advisor. Thank them for their service and ask them if you can say a prayer as a family for their safety. If so, put the phone on speakerphone and say a brief blessing over them as a family.

Option C: Host a Prayer News Night

Ask everyone to pick a prayer-worthy story in the news and share why they care about this subject. It could be a large-scale, ongoing change occurring in society. It may be about a tragedy or natural disaster. It may even be about a mission trip. You might watch the news beforehand, look at the newspaper, or flip through a magazine of current topics with your kids to find prayer-worthy stories.

When ready to pray, ask family members to praise God for His power to guide others who may be in trouble or hurting. Then, go around the room and ask for the news item that is on each person's heart and pray, one by one, for each issue. Then, pray for wisdom and ways to help with these matters, if possible or appropriate. You can even talk more afterward about how you can help. You might like to write letters to soothe hurting hearts, send money to help an organization working with the needy, or plan a family mission trip to aid those in need.

End the activity in prayer for God's bold intervention. Remind your children that prayer is a powerful force for good! Praise Him for what He is about to do. Trust in Him for movement and for His glory to be known.

Community Prayer Activity

Adopt a local mission. Pray about this project throughout your journey, find kid-friendly ways to volunteer within a reasonable time schedule, and document, including photos, your time together. Some local mission ideas include children's homes and foster care coalitions, homeless shelters, pregnancy centers, women's shelters, food pantries, clothes closets, garden ministries, nursing homes and convalescent centers, blood drives, prayer walking, neighborhood clean-ups, backpack and school supply collections, construction projects for the needy, pet fostering and adoption projects, and many more. Check your local white or yellow pages for places to invest in your community.

DEOVTIONAL 8:
PRAYING FOR THOSE WHO ARE SICK

Family Minute

Dear God, we are asking with all of our hearts for Your blessing and great answers. We will give You all the glory for what You do, and we know that You are the Great Physician. Help us, heal us, save us, and love us. In Jesus' holy name, we pray, and we thank You. Amen.

For truly, I say to you, if you have faith like a grain of mustard seed, you will say to this mountain, "Move from here to there," and it will move, and nothing will be impossible for you.

(Matthew 17:20)

True Story from Teresa

My prayer partner Deb Baird has a tremendous healing testimony. Several years ago, she and her husband, Jeff, boarded a plane to Pennsylvania. During the flight, she experienced horrible hemorrhaging. Frantic, she and Jeff exited the flight and hurried to the hospital. There, doctors discovered Deb had a huge tumor as well as a hernia. This meant back-to-back surgeries! The emergency surgeries went well. However, a few days later, she woke up to find her incision had opened and the skin did not look healthy. She contacted the doctor who examined Deb and determined a *third* surgery was necessary.

That night, Deb flew home to gather some belongings and lead a women's study at the church. (Talk about dedication!) She told the group about the upcoming surgery. One lady drew near to her and said, "Deb, I feel like the Lord is impressing upon me to pray over you. I feel in my heart that God is going to heal you."

All of the ladies agreed in prayer, laying hands on Deb and praying with assurance of Matthew 17:20. Deb describes the encounter as "a warm, beautiful feeling of oil being poured over my body." The morning of the surgery, Deb awoke to find that her stomach wound had completely closed and looked normal and healthy.

Still, Deb and Jeff went to the hospital to share what happened. The nurses asked to take her blood pressure and vitals as Deb exclaimed ecstatically, "I believe Jesus healed me! Look at it!" The nurses still insisted on transporting her to surgical preparation. Deb continued to assert, "Please get my doctor. I don't believe I need to have surgery!" Finally, the doctor walked in, a non-believer, and listened skeptically to Deb. "I doubt it's healed," he replied. He carefully inspected the area and then, in disbelief, called in two other doctors. Deb again insisted, "This is a miracle!"

"You got me, Deb. I've never seen anything like this before!" the doctor agreed. "I thought things like this were only supposed to happen in Bible days."

"No, doctor," Deb replied. "Jesus Christ is the same yesterday and today and forever!" (See Hebrews 13:8.) Immediately following the amazing affirmation, one of the nurses asked Deb, "Would you and those same ladies pray for my marriage?" Deb, of course, said yes.[5]

Questions and Thoughts

1. Have you ever had the flu or a cold, feeling really down in the dumps—just awful? You know the kind of sickness—itchy, sneezy, coughing, and aching all over, when you just want to lay in bed and do nothing?

Sometimes even when you feel miserable, small comforts like a cup of chicken noodle soup might help a little. A tender touch or prayer can similarly ease our sufferings.

2. Do you or a family member have a medical condition that you are concerned about?

3. Do you know someone who is suffering right now?

4. Do you get concerned about sicknesses and germs in the world?

We all worry about health sometimes and what the future will be like. But God can take away any sickness, sadness, or sorrows if we only ask Him. Let us have faith in God who is ready and able to move the mountains in your life. Jesus is our one true Healer.

A Simple Prayer for Those Who are Sick

Dear God,

You are the strength for all who love and trust in You. You are the great and mighty Physician, an amazing Healer for those who are sick and needy. Thank You for hearing our prayer today for _____. We trust You to make him/her all better. May his/her sickness turn into good health and joy again.

Through Jesus' powerful name, we pray. Amen.

---

5. Deb Baird is the founder of *God's Own* (www.iamgodsown.com), a speaker, and a pastor's wife.

A Simple Prayer for Your Own Health

Dear God,

Thank You for the life that You have given me. You are my Father, my God, and my Healer. For all of these things, I praise You. Lord, I trust You for my good health to return again. Right now, I don't feel well, but I know that You can make me feel better. I ask You to bring strength to my body, to heal me completely, and to help me to be a testament of Your holy power and love. I pray that You would help me to act loving even when I feel sick. In Jesus' name, I pray, amen.

A Simple Prayer for Family Health

Dear Father in Heaven,

Today, we come before You in the holy name of Jesus Christ, asking for good health for our bodies. We are sick now, and we ask You to make us well. Your holy Word says that by Christ's wounds, we are healed. (See 1 Peter 2:24.) We trust that You hear our prayer, and we will feel much better in no time. Thank You, Lord Jesus! Amen.

A Prayer for a Surgery

Dear Heavenly Father,

Thank You that You are our mighty Healer. We trust in You that _____ will be restored after his/her upcoming surgery. We ask You to guide the doctor's hand who's doing this surgery and to make everything go perfectly. We believe, Lord, that You will give the doctors wisdom as they treat _____ and that soon he/she will be healthy and strong again. Thank You, Jesus!

Praying for a Miracle

Dear Heavenly Father,

You are an amazing God and a powerful Healer. Everything is in Your hands. So, we turn to You today for _____, asking for a miracle of healing. We know that You have all of the ability to heal his/her body even in the condition it is in right now. You are a merciful and amazing God. *"For nothing will be impossible with God"* (Luke 1:37). We trust in Your Word, which says we can ask anything in Your name and You will do it so the Father may be glorified in the Son. We ask today for _____ to be healed completely and for Your glory to shine through. In Jesus' name, we pray and trust. Amen.

Scriptures About Sickness and Healing

(Read through together; consider memorizing one.)

Heal me, O Lord, and I shall be healed; save me, and I shall be saved, for you are my praise.   (Jeremiah 17:14)

Behold, I will bring to it health and healing, and I will heal them and reveal to them abundance of prosperity and security.   (Jeremiah 33:6)

Be not wise in your own eyes; fear the Lord, and turn away from evil. It will be healing to your flesh and refreshment to your bones.   (Proverbs 3:7–8)

…With his wounds we are healed.   (Isaiah 53:5)

He sent out his word and healed them, and delivered them from their destruction.   (Psalm 107:20)

He heals the brokenhearted and binds up their wounds.
(Psalm 147:3)

Beloved, I pray that all may go well with you and that you may be in good health, as it goes well with your soul.   (3 John 2)

They are life to those that find them, and healing to all their flesh.   (Proverbs 4:22)

Ask, and it shall be given you; seek, and ye shall find; knock, and it will be opened to you. (Matthew 7:7)

God's Promises for Our Health

...By keeping all his statutes and his commandments, which I command you, all the days of your life, and that your days may be long. (Deuteronomy 6:2)

With long life I will satisfy him and show him my salvation. (Psalm 91:16)

For by me your days will be multiplied, and years will be added to your life. (Proverbs 9:11)

You shall walk in all the way that the LORD your God has commanded you, that you may live, and that it may go well with you, and that you may live long in the land that you shall possess. (Deuteronomy 5:33)

You shall come to your grave in ripe old age, like a sheaf gathered up in its season. (Job 5:26)

For length of days and years of life and peace they will add to you. (Proverbs 3:2)

For I will restore health to you, and your wounds I will heal. (Jeremiah 30:17)

Interactive Family Prayer

Option A: Take a Hospital Prayer Journey

Take a hospital prayer journey to visit those in the hospital or in a nursing home. Ask your church if anyone is in the hospital who needs a visit. Spend time praying over people who need encouragement. Cheer up those who are hurting or lonely. Sit down as a family after your visit to share one good thing that happened while praying for others.

If you are not able to travel during this time, make prayer phone calls to people in the hospital, in a nursing home, or who are ill. Tell them that you are gathered as a family and would like to pray over them if that's ok. If they say yes, then say a prayer in unison and resolve in a mighty "Amen!" Tell the person that you will continue to pray for them. Or, sit down with your family to write encouraging notes to people who need to be lifted in prayer. Remember these individuals in the days ahead in your family prayers. Write a follow-up prayer card once the person returns home, praying for their continued restoration and healing.

Option B: On-the-Road Medical Prayers

When you're in the car as a family and drive by a hospital, medical center, or doctor's office, take a moment to pray over the doctors, nurses, medical staff, and patients inside. If you see a handicap sticker in the window of a car, pray for that person's health and healing. If you see an ambulance pass you by on the road, pray about the person inside or who may be inside in the future, for perfect healing over their bodies. Pray that the emergency care workers would have wisdom to deliver the best care for that individual.

Option C: Prayer Bookmarks

Google a template for bookmarks online and print them out for all family members. (We liked the ones at https://www.template. net/business/word-templates/blank-bookmark-template/.)   Print the bookmarks on heavy paper or cardstock. Then color, decorate, and design the bookmarks. Make cross ornaments the same way by printing a template, cutting them out, and decorating. Include a short prayer or Scripture on each one. Then, take the bookmarks and/or ornaments to people in the hospital or in nursing homes for a gift of cheer and a "talking point" if you run out of things to say.

Community Prayer Activity

Have a card-making time as a group, and then spend time each writing a small note in the cards to those who are suffering from illness. Gather addresses, and send the card via snail mail. End by praying as a group for the individuals who are sick.

DEVOTIONAL 9:
PRAYING DURING GRIEF AND HARDSHIP

Family Minute

Dear God, You are our Father, Creator, hope, and salvation. Thank You, Jesus, for Your sacrifice for our sins—for dying on the cross and rising again—so that we may have life eternal. Thank You, Prince of Peace, for Your constant comfort and love. We know that things like sickness and death can be frightening, so put all our confidence and faith in You. It's in Your holy name that we pray. Thank You, Jesus. Amen.

For God so loved the world, that he gave his only Son, that whoever believes in him should not perish but have eternal life. (John 3:16)

True Story from Teresa

We are all saddened when watching screen or stage adaptations of the crucifixion of Jesus Christ or reading the original account in the Gospels. It's hard to believe people could ever be so cruel and misunderstanding as they were to Jesus.

He was publicly beaten and whipped before large stake-like nails were driven through His wrists and ankles to attach Him to the cross. There, He hung for six painful hours between two convicted criminals. A mocking inscription placed above His head read, "The King of the Jews." Soldiers shouted mean insults to Him as His blessed mother, Mary, and the disciple John looked on in tears and heartache. From the cross, He spoke to His mother and John. He also cried out in agony to His Father, "My God, my God, why have You forsaken Me?" Darkness covered the land. Jesus then called out in a firm voice, "Father, into Your hands I commit My spirit." An earthquake shook the ground, tearing down the temple. But three days later, after being buried in a dark tomb, Jesus rose from the dead, and His light and life shines for all of us sinners today. (See Matthew 27–28; Mark 15–16; Luke 23–24; John 19–20.)

The crucifixion and brutality of this story pierces our hearts. When we chose to let our children watch *The Jesus Film* from beginning to end, so that they could see how painful life is and yet how great Jesus' love is, the sacrifice of our Savior on the cross brought tears to our daughter's eyes. However, she also recognized that death isn't the end. Because of Christ and His sacrifice, death is, for the Christian, a new beginning. At only four years old, Meyana asked Jesus into her heart and has been one of His biggest cheerleaders ever since. Thankfully, together, we recognize a Savior who loves us, rose again, and lives today!

Questions and Thoughts

1. Have you ever watched or heard the story of Jesus on earth from beginning to end?

2. Does the story of the death of Jesus seem sad? What happened afterward?

The sacrifice of Jesus on the cross can make us sad during the crucifixion, but happy in the end. It's ok to be sad. Even Jesus wept at the tomb of His friend Lazarus. Until Christ comes again and every tear is wiped away, there will be sadness and death on the earth. That's why we look in hope to Christ—who raised Lazarus from the dead, and who Himself was raised from the dead on the third day, defeating death forever!

3. Do you know someone who has passed away? Does the idea of death make you scared? What can you think about when death makes you afraid?

Jesus! He is the key to eternal life so that even in dying, we may live. Because He rose again from the dead, He defeated death—death has no more power! Death is only the gateway to eternal life in Jesus' presence. As you seek Him, may you uncover more about His story and form a bond to carry with you through both good and tough times. Jesus is the key to eternity, love, and joy. Praise Jesus!

A Simple Prayer when Someone You Love Has Died

Dear Heavenly Father,

We are so sad that _____ died. Yet, we know and trust that You are taking good care of him/her in the joyfulness of heaven. Through You, we can dwell in the house of the Lord forever. We pray You will comfort those who loved _____. Help them to have Your peace in their hearts. Surround them with Your love. Let a loving memory of _____ remain in their hearts. Thank You, Jesus. Amen.

Prayer for Someone Who May be Dying

Dear Almighty God,

Thank You for _____'s life and for all that he/she means to many. I pray that You will bring great peace and comfort to

_____. I pray he/she will not be in pain. I pray for rest and assurance that You are with him/her no matter what and that You will lift the burdens of his/her heart. In Jesus' name, I pray. Amen.

Prayer for the Chronically Ill

We pray today for _____ that he/she may know You and trust in You. We pray that if it would be Your will, powerful God, that You would heal _____. We will give You all of the glory, honor, and praise. If it is not Your will to heal _____, we pray that You will be with him/her every moment. Send Your angels to surround him/her. Grant Your peace and serenity. Release the pain from his/her body and make it all better in Your comfort and love. In Jesus' precious name, we trust. Amen.

Scriptures about Our Hope in Christ

(Read through together; consider memorizing one.)

Blessed are those who mourn, for they shall be comforted.
(Matthew 5:4)

Blessed be the God and Father of our Lord Jesus Christ, the Father of mercies and God of all comfort. (2 Corinthians 1:3)

He will wipe away every tear from their eyes, and death shall be no more, neither shall there be mourning, nor crying, nor pain anymore, for the former things have passed away.
(Revelation 21:4)

Even though I walk through the valley of the shadow of death, I will fear no evil, for you are with me; your rod and your staff, they comfort me.   (Psalm 23:4)

Surely goodness and mercy shall follow me all the days of my life, and I shall dwell in the house of the Lord forever.
(Psalm 23:6)

"Blessed are the dead who die in the Lord from now on."
"Blessed indeed," says the Spirit, "that they may rest from their
labors, for their deeds follow them!"   (Revelation 14:13)

Blessed be the God and Father of our Lord Jesus Christ!
According to his great mercy, he has caused us to be born again
to a living hope through the resurrection of Jesus Christ from
the dead.   (1 Peter 1:3)

I have fought the good fight, I have finished the race, I have
kept the faith. Henceforth there is laid up for me the crown of
righteousness, which the Lord, the righteous judge, will award
to me on that Day, and not only to me but also to all who have
loved his appearing.   (2 Timothy 4:7–8)

God's Promises for Our Eternal Life

For God so loved the world, that he gave his only Son, that
whoever believes in him should not perish but have eternal
life.   (John 3:16)

Let not your hearts be troubled. Believe in God; believe also
in me. In my Father's house are many rooms. If it were not so,
would I have told you that I go to prepare a place for you? And
if I go and prepare a place for you, I will come again and will
take you to myself, that where I am you may be also.
                                                 (John 14:1–3)

Jesus said to her, "I am the resurrection and the life. Whoever
believes in me, though he die, yet shall he live, and everyone
who lives and believes in me shall never die. Do you believe
this?"   (John 11:25–26)

Interactive Family Prayer

Option A: Read the Story of Jesus' Crucifixion

Read the story of Jesus' death and resurrection as a family from a Bible storybook or from the Bible. (See Matthew 27–28; Mark 15–16; Luke 23–24; John 19–20.) Matthew 28:1–6 gives a great account of His miraculous resurrection you can read together:

> *Now after the Sabbath, toward the dawn of the first day of the week, Mary Magdalene and the other Mary went to see the tomb. And behold, there was a great earthquake, for an angel of the Lord descended from heaven and came and rolled back the stone and sat on it. His appearance was like lightning, and his clothing white as snow. And for fear of him the guards trembled and became like dead men. But the angel said to the women, "Do not be afraid, for I know that you seek Jesus who was crucified. He is not here, for he has risen, as he said. Come, see the place where he lay."*

Take turns reading. After you talk about Jesus rising and ascending into heaven, read briefly the Scripture about Jesus returning to us: *"For the Son of man shall come in the glory of his Father with his angels; and then he shall reward every man according to his works"* (Matthew 16:27 KJV).

Talk about your belief in Jesus and why you feel the way you do. Describe that all you have to do is tell Jesus you believe in Him, His life, death, resurrection, and the salvation that comes from Him. You can trust that He came to forgive our sins and that He will come again someday. Then, ask Him into your heart forever.

Option B: Gather a Basket

Take a trip to a local health food store and ask each family member to choose one or two items for a basket to bless someone who is ill. Wrap the basket in plastic and attach an envelope of prayer notes from each family member, saying that you hope they get well soon and that you are praying for them.

Option C: Light a Single Candle

When someone you love is very ill or has passed, spend quiet and tender moments as a family lighting a single candle for that person and praying for them, for their family, and for their extended family, too.

Community Prayer Activity

Work with your small or community group to host a quarterly prayer vigil for the sick on a specific date and time. Host this in a focused church location such as a sanctuary or chapel. Open this to anyone in your group or church that needs special prayer over illnesses and concerns. Encourage group members to invite their families and extended families. You could even have sign-up times for five- to ten-minute dedicated prayer times throughout an evening. Offer each attendee a meaningful take-home prayer sheet or booklet. Conclude the evening with simple prayer and soft worship music.

DEVOTIONAL 10:

PRAYING ABOUT SERVING GOD

Family Minute

Dear God, You are the Map for our future. Encourage us to serve You and others as we long for Your perfect will. May our goals be founded upon Your amazing wisdom and objectives. May we obey Your commands as we seek an abundant life and seek out the road ahead. Thank You, Jesus! It's in Your holy and precious name that we pray and trust. Amen.

The heart of man plans his way, but the Lord *establishes his steps.* (Proverbs 16:9)

True Story from Teresa

We all have goals in life, plans for the future—our work, hopes, and dreams. As a kid, my dream was to become a newspaper reporter. I imagined myself as a lead correspondent for the *Dallas Morning News*, on the beat every day writing columns and the latest updates. I even considered being a sports reporter after covering sports in high school and college.

In the real world, however, I realized it wasn't going to happen as easily as I thought. Three different reporters from local newspapers all told me how difficult it was to get a start in the industry. If I wanted to write for a large paper, they said, I needed to work my way up from ad sales. I recall thinking, *I need a Higher Power to help.* I began a career in advertising and marketing instead, but I kept the desire to be a writer. I often jumped at the chance for any report-creating opportunities, to maintain my research and writing skills.

I realized, as time passed, that when we pray about what we wish for, often God will bless our plans. There were a few welcome detours in my career like the adoption of our son and daughter, and soon after, God planted the idea in my heart of an adoption ministry. We began adoption and foster care support efforts to help other families. Then, I felt more inspired than ever to write books for a living. I knew I had plenty of material.

It is clear now that when our hearts are in it—and it is God's will—the Lord establishes each step of the way. I may not have gotten the newspaper reporting job that I daydreamed about, but God led me to an occupation and calling that I'm even more excited about. Thank God for His plan that determines who we are in Jesus!

Questions and Thoughts

1. Do you have specific goals, hopes, or dreams for the future? Maybe you want to be a reporter, a teacher, an architect, a missionary, a preacher, an artist, a doctor, or an astronaut!

Whatever you wish for, you can bring it closer to reality through prayer. In the real world, we have to work hard to achieve our goals. We often require a Higher Power to help. In fact, it's always important that our plans fall in line with God's.

2. Do you have a hope or an intention for your life?

When we pray about what we wish for, God will bless and take care of our goals through His wisdom, care, and love.

3. Is your heart passionate about something? Do you feel a desire to ask for God's help with your track to success?

4. Are you ready to pray for what you desire?

Don't forget to follow God in prayer because He can ensure your victory, while sharing His glory with the world.

A Simple Prayer about Serving God

Dear Heavenly Father,

We praise You, Lord Jesus! We pray that we can serve You well. We pray we can lead others to You. Please forgive our shortcomings. Please keep us in Your light, strength, and grace. Help us to have courage as a family to help others understand Your salvation. Fill us with Your Spirit, peace, and love. Most of all, give us the ability to best serve You as followers of Jesus Christ. May we be faithful to You all the days of our lives. In Jesus' holy name, we pray. Amen.

A Simple Prayer about Serving Others

Dear Heavenly Father,

Thank You for giving us the chance to serve You, Holy God. Thank You for the opportunity to serve others. We hope that by serving, we can teach others all about You. Please enable us to be more like You: full of mercy, without grumbling or complaining, respectful and kind. Let Your Holy Spirit shine through us each day. Help us to assist others in need like the Good Samaritan did long ago. Help us to be like Jesus to those who are hurting or need a hand. We pray that You will lead them closer to You through Your love. In Jesus' name, we pray. Amen.

Scriptures about Serving the Lord and One Another

(Read through together; consider memorizing one.)

Mankind will say, "Surely there is a reward for the righteous; surely there is a God who judges on earth."   (Psalm 58:11)

If anyone serves me, he must follow me; and where I am, there will my servant be also. If anyone serves me, the Father will honor him.   (John 12:26)

You shall serve the LORD your God, and he will bless your bread and your water, and I will take sickness away from among you.   (Exodus 23:25)

You did not choose me, but I chose you and appointed you that you should go and bear fruit and that your fruit should abide, so that whatever you ask the Father in my name, he may give it to you.   (John 15:16)

Blessed is the one you discipline, LORD, the one you teach from your law.   (Psalm 94:12 NIV)

Bear one another's burdens, and so fulfill the law of Christ.   (Galatians 6:2)

Let no one seek his own good, but the good of his neighbor.   (1 Corinthians 10:24)

Do nothing from selfish ambition or conceit, but in humility count others more significant than yourselves. Let each of you look not only to his own interests, but also to the interests of others.   (Philippians 2:3–4)

God's Promises for Our Service

For the LORD God is a sun and shield; the LORD bestows favor and honor. No good thing does he withhold from those who walk uprightly.   (Psalm 84:11)

Rejoice and be glad, for your reward is great in heaven, for so they persecuted the prophets who before you.

(Matthew 5:12)

Oh, fear the LORD, you his saints, for those who fear him have no lack! The young lions suffer want and hunger; but those who seek the LORD lack no good thing.

(Psalm 34:9–10)

But seek first the kingdom of God and his righteousness, and all these things will be added to you.

(Matthew 6:33)

And my God will supply every need of yours according to his riches in glory in Christ Jesus.   (Philippians 4:19)

God…richly provides us with everything to enjoy.

(1 Timothy 6:17)

Interactive Family Prayer

Option A: Create a Family Poem

Have each family member write a prayer poem using any or all of the words below. You can use other terms as well; however, you need to use at least five of the words listed below in your poem.

> God peace faith serving home hope future blessings where time rain year mission helping others praise Jesus born again try team friend family love unity roam scope send dove fear near raise beam why cry heart renew pray pain brothers care sisters wise Christ prize peace bear doing going moving agree believe see understand find trust

Then, ask each person to read their poem aloud. If someone feels uncomfortable with sharing, then offer to read it for them. You may decide you want to save the poems in a family memory book to enjoy later. (You can even do this activity once a year or more and change the words according to the ages of the participants.)

Option B: At-Home Spa

Sometimes serving others means getting our hands dirty—or wet! Jesus knelt to wash the feet of His disciples, a job that was usually left to the lowest of the low servants. Yet here was Jesus, the Master, serving His disciples in a tangible, beautiful way. Act this out in your own family in the spirit of service! Either use an electric foot spa or bath, or create your own in a large steel tub. Add warm water and Epsom salt, and, one at a time, offer each person in the family five to ten minutes in the "spa" and then use warm towels to pat dry their feet. If you have daughters, this is a great time for a pedicure! Next, use a relaxing lavender or sandalwood-type lotion and massage their feet. Then, give them some warm slippers to keep their feet warm, clean, and cozy. While you wash their feet, remind them of how Jesus washed His disciples' feet in John 13:3–10, 14–17:

> *Jesus knew that the Father had put all things under his power, and that he had come from God and was returning to God; so he got up from the meal, took off his outer clothing, and wrapped a towel around his waist. After that, he poured water into a basin and began to wash his disciples' feet, drying them with the towel that was wrapped around him. He came to Simon Peter, who said to him, "Lord, are you going to wash my feet?" Jesus replied, "You do not realize now what I am doing, but later you will understand." "No," said Peter, "you shall never wash my feet." Jesus answered, "Unless I wash you, you have no part with me." "Then, Lord," Simon Peter replied, "not just my feet but my hands and my head as well!" Jesus answered, "Those who have had a bath need only to wash their feet; their whole body is clean.... Now that I, your Lord and Teacher, have washed your feet, you also should wash one*

another's feet. *I have set you an example that you should do as I have done for you. Very truly I tell you, no servant is greater than his master, nor is a messenger greater than the one who sent him. Now that you know these things, you will be blessed if you do them."*   (NIV)

Option C: Captain, My Captain

Discuss five reasons why God is the Leader or Captain of your life and family, such as "we are as lost as sheep without Him," or "He alone guides us in truth." Thank Him in prayer for these things and ask God to show you how to be a better follower of Jesus Christ. If possible, connect this with actually getting out on the water in a boat with your family. You could rent a boat, go canoeing, or go kayaking on a local lake or pond. Alternatively, you could visit a museum that has a display on ships—possibly even offering the chance to tour the ship or boat. Finally, if you children are very small, you can float plastic boats in a kiddie pool or in the bathtub, with a plastic toy as the "captain." After the activity, take time to thank the Captain of the world for directing our lives.

Community Prayer Activity

In the spirit of service, adopt a local charity for a volunteer project. Consider area children's homes or foster families who may need help producing personal care kits for their children. Determine a list of necessary items and ask each group member to collect items for at least two to three kits each. Come together to finalize the kits and deliver them to the local foster care organization or children's home representative. Pray over each bag that you generate for children—that it would bless them and that God would encourage each child with a vision of His plan for the future. Write this Scripture on a card for the recipients: *"For I know the plans I have for you,' declares the Lord, 'plans to prosper you and not to harm you, plans to give you hope and a future'"* (Jeremiah 29:11 NIV).

100 MORE SIMPLE IDEAS FOR FAMILY OR GROUP PRAYER

*C*ongratulations—you have completed the ten focused devotionals and started a valuable habit for you and your family. To continue your new habit, I put together 100 more simple ideas for family or group prayer.

The purpose of these 100 prayer activities is to find ways to recognize God in all aspects of your family life—not just during traditional family devotions, but in every minute, every activity, and every thought, of every day. Let prayer invade your daily life! Some of these activities are ways to jazz up your family prayer time; others are ideas for weekends; still others are passive-engagement activities that can be maintained for days or weeks. Not all of these ideas will fit your family's character or lifestyle—but that's ok! Find one that fits, and run with it! The 100 activities are roughly organized by age-appropriate level, beginning with the youngest ages.

1. Clapping Hands Prayers

Begin the prayer time with ten claps of your hands in unison or in a special rhythm. Whenever somebody wants to pray, they have to clap three times, and then they can pray—either aloud or silently. When they're done, everyone else gets a chance to clap three times in order to pray.

2. Bus Stop Prayers

Stop by your local bus stop and pray for those traveling from place to place.

3. Stop Sign Prayers

Many of us spends hours every week in a car—often with the kids. Incorporate prayer into those moments by playing a game of praying—out loud and even at the same time!—every time you stop at a stop sign. (Driver keeps their eyes open, of course.)

4. Camp-n-Pray

Either go to a physical camping area or set up a fort in the living room and spend time in focused prayer to God. Afterward, share in campfire treats.

5. Snack Time Prayers

Take a break from the busy, fast-paced day. Ask everyone to choose a favorite snack, sit around the dining room table or the living room together, and partake in simple prayers of encouragement.

6. Bedtime Stories

Read a story chosen by your child. Then, talk about the purpose of the story and what you learned from it. (We love reading a different Bible story every night.) Say a prayer for your child to be touched by the lesson of the book and to carry it with them always. Ask the child if there's anything on his or her mind and pray for that, too.

7. Prayer Balloon Release

Buy or inflate helium balloons. Write your prayer request on them with a permanent marker. Then send them up to God in full faith of receiving answers. (Wait for them to rise and pop and watch for where the pieces fall to retrieve them.)

8. Wilderness Prayers

Go on a wilderness journey. Scout out local parks and trails through nature—whether a national park, a local nature habitat, or a trail by a local lake or river. While exploring, rejoice in God's precious outdoors—the birds, trees, flowers, lakes, and rivers. You can Instagram photos of nature's beauty or your family celebrating, and add a Scripture and a prayer to share your love for the Lord. Before leaving, pray that your family will understand the beauty God has created. Unless it's against the guidelines for the area, bring home souvenirs, such as handfuls of dried grass for a vase in your house or shiny rocks to put in a bowl on the coffee table.

9. Bonfire Prayer

Set up a bonfire with wood burning and marshmallows roasting. Ask each family member to bring a small piece of paper with a written prayer request on it. Parents can place the requests carefully into the fire, one by one, and as they go up in smoke, remember that they're symbolic of our prayers lifted up to heaven, prayed with trust in God to take care of everything.

10. Yogurt Stop Prayers

Ask your family members and friends to meet at a frozen yogurt shop for a treat and some dedicated time of prayer. This changes up the prayer time so it doesn't get monotonous for kids.

11. Origami Prayer

Write out your prayer request with a marker or crayon on a piece of colorful paper. Then fold the paper into an origami pattern—or an airplane, or whatever comes to mind! For easy origami instructions, visit: www.origami-instructions.com/simple-origami. Then, put your origami creations somewhere handy where they can be used as a visual aid to remind children of a certain prayer request.

12. Flashlight Prayer

Gather in a candlelit room with flashlights for each family member. If someone wants to pray, they flash the flashlight on and off, say their prayer, and then pick which person can pray next.

13. Jumpstart Your Prayer

Get a child's jump rope and utilize your exercise time as a family to take turns jumping rope and praying for at least one area each as a family. Whoever jumps, prays. Then the next person goes and so on. It's a great way to remind your kids that God hears our words no matter what we're doing—He hears when we sit quietly with bowed head and folded hands but also when we're jumping, laughing, and goofing off!

14. Farmer-Focused Prayers

Pray for a local farmer, that he/she would have an abundant crop. Season permitting, attend a local farmer's market and buy one vegetable or fruit to eat that your family hasn't tried before. Challenge everyone to try it—and rejoice in the Lord's bountiful creation.

15. Time's Up! Prayer

Bring a bell or chime to your family/group prayer session. Each person has one minute to pray about what's on their heart. Then the leader rings the bell or chime and the prayer rotates to the next person.

16. Tossing Around Prayer

Get a large rubber ball and use a permanent marker to write prayer topics all over the ball, such as praise, family, weather, peace, church, school, or friends. Then, play toss! Whoever catches the ball has to shout out a one-sentence prayer on the topic that their right hand touches, and then they toss the ball on to whomever they want.

17. Message in the Bottle Prayers

With simple, thin strips of paper, write your prayers and favorite Scriptures. Then, place them inside a biodegradable container—paper boat, origami box—and float them down a common river or waterway. Or tuck them away in a family trunk and get them out in the future and see how God has answered those prayers.

18. Make a Prayer Rock Paperweight

Find a rock outside, the size of an apple or grapefruit. Wash it, polish it, and decorate it. Write your family name on it, followed with "PRAYER ROCK." Then, place prayer requests under it as a sort of personal prayer paperweight. As prayers are removed, you can see the weight literally lifted away to God. Thank You, Jesus!

19. Prayers from a Hat

Have everyone write prayer requests and concerns on a slip of paper throughout the week and place them in a hat in the center of a main table of your home. At a given point in the week, everyone gathers together and prays over the requests, tipping your hat to the God who made you.

20. Neighborhood Prayer Walk

Although these days it's normal for neighbors to keep to themselves, it's important to reach out in prayer to bless our neighbors. Gather everyone for a walk through your neighborhood, praying for every home you pass. Pray for unity, for peace, for safety, for an interest or growth in understanding in the gospel, and for a chance to interact with the individuals inside.

21. Make Prayer Cloths

Go to a local hobby or craft store and pick up some of the blank, white, or light-colored handkerchiefs. Draw a design, such as a cross, or write out a Scripture on the cloth with a fabric marker.

Ask your pastor to anoint the cloths with oil. Pray over the cloths and send to them to those who need extra prayer support.

22. Circle of Love

Gather the family in a circle and describe one thing you love about each other. Then, pray for each other and ask the Lord that each family member's spiritual gifts would manifest for God's purposes.

23. Family Theme Song

During family prayer time, have everyone write down what their favorite prayer song is. Then, take a vote (no one is allowed to vote for their own), and whichever song "wins" becomes the family theme song for the week, month, or year! Have everyone pray for God to touch your lives each time you sing or listen to it.

24. Stargazing Prayers

One of our favorite family activities is stargazing. Just grab a blanket and go outside when the sky is dark and filled with His amazing stars shining brightly. Lay down and look up at all God has created in the universe and pray for God's amazing ways to work in and through your lives.

25. Bring a Bible Night

Ask each family member to bring a Bible, read their favorite Scripture, and explain why it's important to them. Pray before and after sharing favorite Scriptures.

26. Hold a Soaking Prayer Meeting

No, not with water, but with prayer! Schedule a specific time (maybe after dinner) for a thirty-minute soaking prayer time for one family member—a time of dedicated prayer over their concerns and heart desires while you enter into God's presence, allowing His love to shine through your prayers of pure love and faith.

27. Library Prayers

If you are regular visitors to your local library, pray over it. Then, gather some cards and write thank-you notes to the librarians, expressing appreciation for their helpfulness, resourcefulness, and caring ways. Hand them to the librarians behind the desk.

28. Crafter's Prayers

Join a local craft meeting and get to know its members while enjoying the crafting time. When you go home, pray over the names of the people you met. If appropriate, ask them for their prayer needs and offer to pray over them.

29. Skittles Prayers

Use Skittles to focus your family prayers. Pass around a bowl of Skittles during your regular prayer meeting. Each person takes a handful, but nobody's allowed to eat them yet! First, explain that the colors of the candy pieces represent the characteristics of the fruit of the Spirit and Christ's love.

> But the fruit of the Spirit is love, joy, peace, patience, kindness, goodness, faithfulness, gentleness, self-control; against such things there is no law. And those who belong to Christ Jesus have crucified the flesh with its passions and desires. (Galatians 5:22–24)

Red Skittles: the love and joy of Jesus that He gave to us by shedding blood on the cross.

Green Skittles: peace and patience, like lying down in green pastures.

Orange Skittles: kindness, like a warm orange bonfire that warms us and others.

Yellow Skittles: goodness and faithfulness, like the sun which is good and faithfully rises each day.

Purple Skittles: gentleness and self-control, like a good king or queen on the throne.

Take a Skittle, say the fruit of the Spirit it represents, and then everyone can eat that color! Pray that the family would obtain the fruit of the Spirit represented. Notice that not everyone has the same amount of each color! This demonstrates that some of the fruits of the Spirit come more naturally to us, but some are more difficult. However, we're called to have each one. Then move on to other colors and fruits of the Spirit.

30. School and Scripture

During family prayer time, focus on 1 John 3:1 for your children. Read and learn this Scripture together: *"See what kind of love the Father has given to us, that we should be called children of God; and so we are."* Spend ten to fifteen minutes with the students in your family writing thank you cards or thank you email messages for their special teachers and faculty. Pray 1 John 3:14–15 about keeping good hearts toward our friends, teachers, and fellow students at school so that we can be better brothers and sisters in Christ. Pray that lost souls will be saved. Remind your kids of the importance of encouraging those in authority.

31. Income-Building Prayers

If you give your children an allowance, consider having them tithe ten percent to the church—as a habit for the years to come—reminding them of the Malachi 3:10–11 message. As you hand out their allowance, whether it's a weekly event or a one-time event, pray for success in your careers, your income-building, your tithing for Christ and His church, and your children's education and future careers.

32. Family Reading Night

Ask every family member to choose his or her favorite story, magazine article, or devotional and bring it to the living room for a family reading night. Pray before and after the reading time.

33. Clean for a Cause Saturday

Choose a cause and clean out items from your house that you could donate to the cause, such as used clothing to Goodwill or Salvation Army, books for men's or women's shelters, or canned goods for the local food pantry. After you've piled it all into the vehicle, take a moment to stand by it and say a quick prayer that the goods would be a blessing to people in need.

34. Scripture Sunday

Hold a weekly five- or ten-minute Scripture memorization time and memorize the same Scripture verse as a family (see chapter 13 for some great ideas). Then, pray this Scripture over those you love.

35. Church Leader Night

Invite a pastor or church staff member to dinner one evening. Ask about what their jobs are like; perhaps even "assign" questions to each child such as: "What's your favorite part of your job?" "How did you come to your current job?" "What are the difficult parts of your job?" "How can we lift you up in prayer?" Spend some time afterward praying about the specific needs.

36. Grocery Store Servants

On your next visit to the local grocery store, let someone go in front of you in line who may be in a hurry or have fewer items than you do. Later, at home, say a prayer as a family for that individual. Remind your children that there are no "chance encounters" with strangers, but rather that God puts each stranger and each person in our lives for a purpose—that we can show forth His love to them!

37. Prayer Wall

Buy a colorful poster board or bulletin board from your local office supply store and place it in a common area of your home. Beside it, leave markers, crayons, or colored pencils where family members can draw or post photos of their prayer needs, thoughts on their mind, or concerns of their heart. It could also include photos cut out from a magazine, articles, photos from a newspaper, inspirational quotes, etc. Remind everyone that they can post to it whenever they want. Place it somewhere eye-catching, like above the kitchen sink or in the bathroom. At the end of the week, sit down, review the poster, ask for further explanations of requests if necessary, and pray over each post.

38. Poetry or Prayer Rap

Sit for a few moments together as a family writing a poem of prayer spontaneously, sort of like making up a rap. One person says a line, then the next person offers another line that rhymes with it, and so on until you have a complete family poem or prayer rap. Write each line on paper or record on a mobile device as words are said aloud. At the end, read or play the poem back to your family. Show everyone how creative you can be as a team in Christ.

39. Praying over Local, State, and Federal Governments

Gather together to pray for peace in our communities, regions, and nation. Contact a local governmental representative, senator, or mayor, and let them know that you're praying for them.

40. Visual Prayer Reminders

Create hearts or crosses from construction paper or other household materials. Write on them the prayer needs of your family's heart. Then, place them in unlikely places like the bathroom or laundry area that will remind you regularly to pray. Consider adding catchphrases such as, "Your Word is sweeter than honey" and "You are the salt of the world" in the kitchen; "Don't just look in the mirror and go away, but be a doer of the Word," on the bathroom mirror, and so on.

41. Create a Thanksgiving Jar

Find a large or medium-sized jar (you can recycle one from your kitchen!) and place it in a common area next to a stack of papers and a few pens. Make a goal to, each day, write down something you're thankful for—whether it's life-changing like "salvation," or simple like "peanut butter." If it's approaching the holiday, you can use orange, red, and brown colored paper, and maybe even glue fallen leaves on the front or add a Scripture about thanksgiving to the jar's label. You could gather together at some point, read the papers, and try to guess who wrote what!

42. Prayer in the Park

Take note of the time of your local sunset. Make a trip to visit a park in the evening to see the sunset—or at least the lengthening shadows! Bring iced tea, juice or lemonade, fruit, crackers and cheese, and mini sandwiches or appetizers to everyone as a fun picnic. Take a few minutes to thank God for His beautiful creation. As the sun drops, pray about areas of your life and concerns you are releasing as a family to God. When the sun is set, thank God for all He is able to do in your family's life. *Or*, wake up early, twenty minutes before sunrise, and hold a focused family prayer time as the sun is rising. What a beautiful experience for all to witness and remember God's powerful majesty together!

43. Pie and Prayer

Everyone pick out a treat at the store or family bakery, or bake your own. Then, have a time of dessert, coffee or tea for parents, and juice for the kids. Discuss your prayer petitions, how God has blessed you, and how you hope to bring glory to Him as a family.

44. Gifts and Talents Prayer

Go around the table or room and have each family member say one favorite hobby. Pray that your family's hobbies will glorify

God. Pray for ways that God can work through you and your hobbies to magnify Him. Pray through this Scripture and ask for God to bless you with His special gifts and talents throughout your family and your lives: *"As each has received a gift, use it to serve one another, as good stewards of God's varied grace: whoever speaks, as one who speaks oracles of God; whoever serves, as one who serves by the strength that God supplies—in order that in everything God may be glorified through Jesus Christ. To him belong glory and dominion forever and ever. Amen"* (1 Peter 4:10–11).

45. Record Your Vision

Print or email Habakkuk 2:2–3 to your family members: *"And the LORD answered me: 'Write the vision; make it plain on tablets, so he may run who reads it. For still the vision awaits its appointed time; it hastens to the end—it will not lie. If it seems slow, wait for it; it will surely come; it will not delay.'"* Ask them to read it and take a few days to write their personal and family goals they are praying to achieve. Then, come together to read the Scripture and share visions and thoughts about this power promise in God's Word.

46. Apostles' Prayer Twitter Party

Examples like Paul's in Acts reminds us the critical importance of praying together. Form a "Prayer Twitter Party" online. First, tweet about your party along with time, date, and details. Choose a party hashtag and include it in your invitation tweets. Ask everyone to bring one praise and prayer to the online event. Then, go to www.5minutesformom.com/twitterparty/ to learn more about setting up and conducting the party.

47. Church Parking Lot Prayers

Drive to church at a time when the parking lot will be mostly empty, and pray for the church. Pray for the unsaved. Pray for those who attend church regularly and irregularly. Pray for the church staff and pastors for God to work and speak through them. Pray for the lawn crews, church volunteers, ministries, and support groups—that all would be successful in serving for His kingdom.

48. Host a Mission Trip Prayer Night and Fundraiser

Host a prayer night or fundraiser for a local missionary leaving on a mission trip. Have an open house format and offer appetizers, snacks, desserts, tea, coffee, and punch. Ask attendees to bring a five or ten dollar bill to help fund the mission. Consider offering door prizes, a special speaker, Christian band, silent auction, or other incentives to attend the evening. Spend a focused time in prayer for the mission, praying that it would be successful to God's great glory.

49. I Will Not Leave You as Orphans

Collect items for orphans, pray over each item to bless the children, and mail them via a reputable orphan rescue organization such as Show Hope or Buckner International. Consider sending diapers to orphans via showhope.org/restore-hope/care-centers/diapers-for-orphans/ or shoes to those in need via www.shoesfororphansouls.com/.

50. Adopt a Local Children's Home

Collect items for children's Christmas gifts and write prayer notes to accompany your gifts of love. Go online to www.samaritanspurse.org/what-we-do/operation-christmas-child/ to learn how. Alternatively, if you know a family in need who would appreciate gifts for their children, consider gathering together Christmas gifts and delivering them personally!

51. Church Blessings—Beyond the Walls Prayers

Spend a night walking in and out of your church, praying for members, pastors, elder, deacons, staff, and attendees by name to be blessed and covered faithfully by the blood and love of Jesus in their daily lives as they go about their week.

52. Post a Prayer

Craft a prayer together to post on Facebook or other social media. Ask each member to contribute at least one line to the prayer message, and end with an invite for others to pray for specific causes—orphans, veterans, shelter animals, and so on.

53. Individual Blessings Prayers

Sometimes it's hard to express faith when you're in a public setting—it's far easier when you're safe inside your house! To build habits of speaking of God wherever you are, have your children say "God bless you" to someone in public on a trip to the grocery store or a movie theater. Encourage them that this is not an opportunity to be outspoken, nor is it necessary to say to everybody all the time, but it can be a great way to subtly acknowledge the Lord in an everyday conversation. Your child could open the door for someone, and if thanked, respond with, "You're welcome; God bless you!" Or they could put someone's grocery cart back in the corral for them, and respond with the same if thanked.

54. Make Your Own Set of Prayer Cards

Sit down with your kids and pull out seven index cards. For each card, write an area of prayer focus at the top, such as worship, confession, thanksgiving, spiritual growth, trials and tribulations, prayer for the lost/salvation prayers, prayers of family protection, or prayers of surrender. Then, for each card, add subtopics. For example, under "worship" you could add, "God's wonderful creation." Under family protection, you could add, "Our vacation plans." Then, when you gather for prayer time, you can "deal" out the cards so that everyone has one or two to pray through.

55. Trusting God's Plan

Research as a family a list of your favorite Scriptures specifically related to facing life's trials. Have each person pick at least one Scripture to write out, pray over, and put in a jar in a family space. Then, the next time somebody is under stress, is frustrated, or is facing a difficult time, remind them to pull a verse out of the jar. Here are a few to look up and get you started: Psalm 91; 1 Peter 5:10; James 1:12; 1 Corinthians 10:13; and John 16:33.

56. Abraham Blessing Prayers

God has a plan for the head of each household to thrive and prosper as descendants of Abraham. Pray over the head of your home, for provision, for peace, and for blessings as they lead your family's day-to-day activities. Consider praying this blessing over the head of the household: *"The LORD bless you and keep you; the LORD make his face to shine upon you and be gracious to you; the LORD lift up his countenance upon you and give you peace"* (Numbers 6:24–26).

57. Identity in Christ Prayers

Especially around Valentine's Day, research as a family a list of your favorite Scriptures that speak explicitly of God's love for His followers. Have each person bring at least one Scripture to pray over, contribute to the prayer session, and remind everyone of God's great love. Here are a few to look up and get you started: John 3:16; Isaiah 40:11; Psalm 100:3; Romans 5:8; and Ephesians 2:4–5.

58. Quiet Time Prayers

Have each family member spend thirty to forty minutes alone in their own room or in a quiet setting, praying and worshipping from his or her heart. Remember Matthew 6:6: *"But when you pray, go into your room, close the door and pray to your Father, who is unseen. Then your Father, who sees what is done in secret, will reward you"* (NIV).

59. Spirit-Led Prayers

Spend moments talking about the Holy Spirit, who He is, and what He means to your family. Read what Romans 8:11 and 8:26 have to say about the Spirit. Ask the Holy Spirit to come in and bless your family with a Spirit-led prayer session.

60. Backyard Prayers

Spend an evening in your backyard with family. Host a barbecue and play a few games like catch or kickball. Then, form a circle around a picnic or foldout table and pray a simple prayer of thanks for good weather, good food, the joy of family, and the fun of being together.

61. Action Jackson Praying

Is there something you've been holding off doing in your life as a family? Maybe a home renovation project—or even a dreamed-of vacation? Initiate a plan of action now. Form specific action steps, agree upon an Action Jackson plan, and pray over it. Then, get to work making that dream a reality, praying for God's blessing over its attainment.

62. Conversational Prayers

Spend a night in conversational prayer. Agree in prayer and thanksgiving as a family that you will be lifting certain thoughts on your mind in a loving, conversational style to God, talking to Him as your Father. Try keeping your eyes open and addressing Him as if He were seated on the couch—with reverence, but also with familiarity. Open your hearts to a whole new meaning as you pray through this amazing method.

63. Directional Prayers

Do you have a time as a family when you talk about plans and schedules for the week, month, or year ahead? If so, use it as a chance to also pray through that plan or schedule—pray for the direction you are going in life, for programs, for school events, for work meetings, and for family goals. Pray that you would, as a family, learn from past events and do well in future events. Pray for trust in God to make all of the directions of your life purposeful and meaningful with Him as your incredible Guide.

64. Pizza Power Prayers

Buy a pre-made pizza crust or make one from scratch. Separate into small, individual round pizza crusts. Then, lay out the sauce, cheese, and a variety of toppings like sausage, veggies, pepperoni, pineapple, etc. Ask everyone to step up to put their choice toppings on their pizza. As they add toppings, ask them to say one perfect power God has over their lives—for example: healing, blessing, or loving them. Then, ask them to lift one prayer to God as they top off the rest of their pizza. Then, the next family member goes, and so on. Bake the pizzas. Then, bon appétit!

65. World Peace Prayers

Find a world map or retrieve an old spinning globe (or "earth ball," as my daughter used to call it). Beside it, stack post-it notes. What is going on in the world today? Wars? Murders? Catastrophes? As you or your family hear of prayer concerns in a particular region of the world, write a post-it note for that area. Post the note where it belongs on the globe. Pray that believers in that region would have strength, peace, and faith; that the governments in those regions would act justly; and that unbelievers in those regions would be humbled before God. Place those petitions before our God and our Savior who alone can bring peace.

66. Missionary Guest Speaker

Invite a missionary from your church or a local ministry. Ask them to tell your family or group about their endeavors for the Lord and to also share specific prayer needs. Lay hands on them during your prayer session and pray for God's power to be at work in their lives. Adopt this person or family to pray about regularly.

67. Worship Night

Ask each family member to bring their favorite worship music song, playlist, or album for a night of singing and praising the Lord. If they are musically gifted, have them lead a time of worship. Give your children practice in leadership by letting them pick the songs and music.

68. Adopt a Soldier

Ask each family member if they know someone in the military they can adopt and pray about. Contact the soldier, through email or snail mail, and ask him/her about how things are going and what their special prayer needs are. Pray over those needs. Check back regularly with this person through letters, phone calls, emails, and special communications during the holidays. You may even want to put together a gift box for special occasions with homemade cookies or other goodies to cheer him/her.

69. "Adopt" an Inmate or Inmate's Child

Jesus says in Matthew 25:36, 40, "*I was in prison and you came to visit me…. I tell you the truth, whatever you did for one of the least of these brothers and sisters of mine, you did for me*" (NIV). Is there a prison ministry in your area? Consider aiding it. Another way to visit a prisoner's heart is to "adopt" their child, sharing love with their little loved one. Go online to www.prisonfellowship.org for more information on how you can help via the Angel Tree Network.

70. Inspirational Leaders Prayer

Have everyone think of a leader who has inspired them. Come together and share stories and then pray for God's inspiration, wisdom, and strength to flow through you to accomplish great things for His kingdom.

71. Testimonial Praise and Prayer

Share with the kids your personal testimony: How did God rescue you? When? How? Tell about how He has worked in your lives and/or your marriage. Then, ask each child to think about their personal testimony and begin shaping their testimony as he or she grows. Ask them what God has done for them already in their lives. No matter what their age, this is a great team-building exercise to strengthen faith and family unity.

72. Praying the Psalms

The book of Psalms in the Bible is a book of prayers. There are prayers of thanks, prayers of praise, and prayers of asking for forgiveness. There are messages about overcoming obstacles like temptation, fear, or discouragement. There are prayers about seeking wisdom and gaining strength in Christ when courage is necessary. Read a psalm and then pray through it, using the psalmist's words but also adding to them as you are moved or as is appropriate. Praying the message behind the psalm is a great way to communicate lovingly and openly with God. Go online to www.psalm119association.org/The-Psalms.html to obtain some wonderful resources on the Psalms for your family.

73. Fast-n-Pray

Teach your children the importance of giving up certain food items for the purpose of seeking answered prayer and God's glory. Perhaps for the season of Lent, or for any day, week, or month of the year that seems appropriate, decide as a family to give up a certain nonessential food, such as soda, candy, or bread. Explain that every time they crave the food, they can view it as a reminder from the Lord to love spiritual things more than material (although we are always to take care of our bodies' needs!). A craving becomes a sort of alarm clock to remind our bodies to go before the Lord in prayer.

74. Comedy Night

Ask each family or group member to bring their favorite joke (keep it clean!) to the prayer meeting. They may have to check out a family joke book or some Christian comedians to find one. (Some of our favorite jokes come from Tim Hawkins.) During the session, ask them to share their joke or comedy routine. Pray afterward for your family's joy and happiness to continue forevermore in Christ.

75. Prayer Partners

Divide your family into prayer partner teams of two. Ask them to have some candid talks about what's going on in their lives and areas where they need additional prayer. After the talk, ask them to pray for each other, then to keep in touch about their prayer updates.

76. Sports Night Prayers

If you have an important upcoming football, baseball, volleyball, soccer, or other sports game, decide to gather fifteen to twenty minutes beforehand so that you can pray on location over the teams involved. Pray for no injuries, for a good, happy, blessed game, and for the peace and joy of the teams and players. Ultimately, agree in prayer that God would be glorified through this event.

77. Prayer Chain

Build a family counsel chain of prayer warriors that you can extend your family prayer needs to and vice versa. You can do this via email, mail, or phone, or by joining together in person, but it's a great way to extend your circle of prayer.

78. Circle of Gratitude

Form a circle as a family. Circles represent unbrokenness, unity, and love. Go around the room and say three things you are grateful to God for and why. Then, say a praise and thanksgiving to God for being so wonderful to your family.

79. Occupational Prayers

Is there a specific profession mom or dad are involved in? Pray for their success and abundant blessings in their careers, and that the family would be able to tithe well to Jesus' church. Then, ask the children what they wish to be when they grow up and pray that they would be full of God's great honor and praise, for full success in getting there (if it requires college or special training), and for God's reinforcement and help along the way.

80. Scripture Card Prayer

Make a set of Scripture card prayers. Either cut some heavy cardstock to card-size or purchase some index cards, and type or write favorite Scripture verses on them. Use them to memorize the verses, kind of like flashcards. Then, say a prayer after rehearsing each one.

81. DVD Prayer

Check out a Christian-based film from your church or local library that you can watch together as a family. Some ideas are: *Heaven Is for Real, The Ultimate Life, Amazing Grace, Courageous, Brother White, War Room,* or *Facing the Giants.* After you watch the movie, stop and pray for God to encourage you to do something great just for Him.

82. Prescription Prayers

Have each person brings the most pressing prayer need they have to the family circle. Then, as a family, determine one Scripture in the Bible that addresses that need, and pray over the need with the added Scripture prescription.

83. Game Night Prayers

Host a family game night. Play charades, Bible trivia, or some other game related to the Bible. Then, say a prayer for your family to grow closer to God's plan and Word.

84. Prayer Garden

Consider starting your own small or large prayer garden with your favorite wildflowers, fruits, or veggies. Add a bench to the area where prayer can be lifted anytime a family member wishes.

85. "Give Me That Old Time Religion"

Do you have a song from an old hymnal that touches your heart? If your kids don't know these songs, take a moment to print some from the internet or visit a local music store to get a guide to the classic hymns. Then sing a few of the songs together and spend time afterward in prayer.

86. Curfew Prayers

Consider praying with your children as they return home for the evening at curfew. Offer them gentle reminders of your love and God's love over them, offer safety prayers, or offer prayers of hope for the future. This is also a good opportunity to ask your teen to share anything that may be weighing on their mind or heart.

87. Disciple Night

Host a disciple night where you study the characteristics of the disciples. Recall the Scripture, "*The disciples went and did as Jesus had directed them*" (Matthew 21:6), and discuss what particular attributes the disciples had that made them true followers of Jesus. For additional information about Jesus' followers and their attributes, visit www.crossroad.to/HisWord/verses/topics/disciples.htm.

88. Wise Solomon Prayers

Is there a big decision ahead of your family or of a member of your family? Maybe a decision about a job, or about which college to go to, or whether to play a specific sport in the upcoming school year. Before praying for wisdom about the decision, read about Solomon's dream in 1 Kings 3.

The LORD *appeared to Solomon in a dream by night, and God said, "Ask what I shall give you." And Solomon said, "…Give your servant therefore an understanding mind to govern your people, that I may discern between good and evil, for who is able to govern this your great people?"*

It pleased the Lord that Solomon had asked this. And God said to him,

"Because you have asked this, and have not asked for yourself long life or riches or the life of your enemies, but have asked for yourself understanding to discern what is right, behold, I now do according to your word. Behold, I give you a wise and discerning mind, so that none like you has been before you and none like you shall arise after you. I give you also what you have not asked, both riches and honor, so that no other king shall compare with you, all your days. And if you will walk in my ways, keeping my statutes and my commandments, as your father David walked, then I will lengthen your days."

(1 Kings 3:5–6, 9–14)

Then, pray for God's wisdom and favor over your family, just as He showed to Solomon.

89. Generosity Prayers

Think of one way you can bless another person with your generosity. It may not be about your money, but about your time, effort, gifts, baking, drawing, or other skills and talents. Take that time to graciously give to the person or people you instinctively have in mind, as a family. Pray before you act, and God will bless you abundantly.

90. Prayer Room

Do you have a home office or special room that is separate from all common rooms of the house? If so, designate that space as a prayer room for a week and put a Bible there. Anytime someone has a prayer need, they can go to that room and pray in solitude or together with others.

91. Family Blog for God

Brainstorm together about your family's major answered prayers from God. Write about the journey to get to those answers and how God ultimately answered the hopes of your family. Then, share it online as a blog or Facebook post for others to be encouraged. Pray that the unsaved will be impacted and saved just through reading your family's post.

92. Pinterest Prayers

If you have a child who enjoys cruising Pinterest, create your own themed Pinterest prayer board together. Go online to www.pinterest.com/anniejobee/prayers-strength-quotes/ for a great example.

93. Write a Family Values Plan

Include your top five family values and why they are important to each of you and pray that your family would incorporate those values in every moment of your lives.

94. "Why I Believe" Dinner and Discussion

Host a special night of talking as a family about why you believe in God, who Jesus is to you, and why you trust in His power.

95. Rotating Themes

The eldest of the family picks a theme for prayer and holds a ten-to-fifteen minute prayer time about that theme. Then, the next oldest person in line picks the next prayer theme for the following session on a different day and so on.

96. Write a Prayer Letter

Is there a friend who needs prayer? Write a prayer letter to them as a family. Start by drafting an email or consider hand writing on a printed stationery sheet for more impact. Begin the letter by saying a simple hello and explaining that you're sending a prayer letter. Then, have each family member write out a prayer—short and sweet or long and thoughtful, either is ok—and record or sign their name beneath the prayer. Close by encouraging your friend to let you know when God answers the prayer and to keep in touch however best fits their communications.

97. Salvation Prayer Night

Hold a prayer time dedicated to praying for unsaved friends and family members, and ask fellow believers to come with a list of people to pray for. Spend the prayer time focusing on prayers for the salvation of these particular individuals. Place the list of names in a file folder to revisit in prayer regularly.

98. Biblical Oils/Herbs and Prayer

Did you know that there are many oils and herbs mentioned throughout the Bible that can help you in the healing process? For example, frankincense can be used to strengthen the immune system. Myrrh is a powerful antioxidant that has antibacterial, antifungal, and anti-parasitic functions. Hyssop, mentioned in Psalm 51:7, can relieve muscle spasms, cramps, rheumatism, and arthritis. Go to a health foods store, either real or virtual, and purchase one of the herbs mentioned in the Bible. Then, gather the family to taste and smell the herb and to look up each verse where it's mentioned in the Bible. Say a prayer of thanks that we're still "close" to the events mentioned in the Bible; that even though they happened a long time ago, they didn't occur in a different world; and that everything in the Bible is true and real to life.

99. Road Trip

Map out a road trip—it could be to a nearby park, a weekend trip, or even to your summer vacation destination. Then, show everyone a map and vote on stops to make along the way to your destination. Pinpoint those stops on the map. When it's time to leave for vacation, pray for a safe journey and thank God for the time away. When you stop on the way to your destination, spend a few moments to fill up, not just on food and gas, but on praises to God!

100. Begin Again Prayers

Is there something that you failed at in life? If so, pick up the pieces together and determine ways to try again. Together as a family, pray over the next steps and go for your hopes and dreams.

PRAYERS FOR HOLIDAYS AND SPECIAL OCCASIONS

We don't need special words to address our God. Thank goodness! He is ready and willing to hear our every prayer when our hearts are directed to Him. However, sometimes it's nice to have somewhere to start when praying for special occasions. (And, of course, because I'm me, you'll notice that my special occasions include days to celebrate children and pets!) Here is your diving board, so that you can jump into your year with a prayer sample for every holiday and other big events.

January

New Year's

Powerful God of the Universe,

We come to You in this amazing new year, trusting for a good, prosperous, and happy year ahead, asking You for warm and awesome connections with family, strength and harmony in relationships, and humility and openness to sustain us on Your path to the future. We ask that our goals for the year would be about You, serving and offering loving sacrifices of joy, hope, peace, and adoration in all we do. With Your great help and guidance, we trust we can be pillars of Christ-like love in the community. Thank You, Jesus! It's in Your holy name that we pray and trust. Amen.

Chinese New Year

Thank You, Lord, for all Your precious believers who are celebrating Chinese New Year today; may their hearts be blessed as we celebrate in joy the diversity of our cultures. Thank You for all the children from the Chinese culture who are now living in adoptive homes in America. Although we celebrate in the New Year in different ways, we all celebrate the same points in our lives—our families, our hopes, our dreams, our faith, and our joys. Let those who know You, Lord, know You more in complete happiness and faithfulness. Let those who don't know You, realize Your salvation and celebrate Your great and omnipresent ways most of all. Thank You, Jesus! Praise You, Jesus, forevermore!

Martin Luther King (MLK) Day (3rd Monday of Jan.)

God of Justice,

Bless the memory and the work of Dr. Martin Luther King. May his labors carry on through those who cherish Your people. May there be a light of hope and influential teaching of compassion in our schools, churches, communities, nation, and world. May there be a spirit of unity. May there be cooperation among all people resting on common democracy and peace. May the American dream be available and within reach of all classes, races, and ethnicities in our communities. May we experience liberty, civil rights, and justice for all, as our Constitution clearly states and as MLK stood for in this vital cause. We are all Your people, so may we strive most significantly for You, God, believing that Your sovereignty is above all and sacred. We strive now for Your good will, order, peace, freedom, and prosperity for our neighbors. No matter what race, color, or creed, we are all one in God's grace. In Jesus' precious and most high and holy name we pray, amen.

February

Valentine's Day (February 14)

Lord, Our Loving Heavenly Father,

Thank You for Your love! And thank You for teaching us about love through Your example. Lord, don't let us be noisy gongs or clanging cymbals. Let us speak everything in love. Let us act everything in love. Please help us to be patient and kind; help us to neither envy nor boast. May we not be arrogant and rude, nor insist on having things our own way. Protect us from irritation and resentment. Instead of rejoicing at wrongdoing, may we always, only, ever rejoice in the truth! Help us to bear all things, believe all things, hope all things, and endure all things. Lord, You *are* love. Teach us to love like You. In Your matchless name, amen.

(For the inspiration of this prayer, see 1 Corinthians 13.)

March

St. Patrick's Day (March 17)

Dear Loving Father,

Thank You for sending St. Patrick to preach about Your kingdom to the people of Ireland. Today, we march on to reach the unsaved for Your glory. As St. Patrick proclaimed Your great love toward all men and women, may we also extend Your message far and wide, here and globally. May Your promise reach those who are lost, surrounding them with Your steadfast light. May those who remain for You live more confidently with a keen ability to share and give testimony. May Your love and serenity reign in our hearts as we move onward as the Holy Spirit guides us. Thank You that You are our one true God! We praise You in Jesus' holy name. Amen.

Legend has it that St. Patrick composed this prayer in AD *433:*

I arise today, through God's strength to pilot me: God's might to uphold me, God's wisdom to guide me, God's eye to look before me, God's ear to hear me, God's word to speak for me, God's hand to guard me, God's way to lie before me, God's shield to protect me, God's host to secure me: against snares of devils, against temptations of vices, against inclinations of nature, against everyone who shall wish me ill, afar and anear, alone and in a crowd.

I summon today all these powers between me and these evils: against every cruel and merciless power that may oppose my body and my soul, against incantations of false prophets, against black laws of heathenry, against false laws of heretics, against craft of idolatry, against spells of witches, smiths, and wizards, against every knowledge that endangers man's body and soul. Christ to protect me today against poisoning, against burning, against drowning, against wounding, so that there may come abundance in reward.

Christ with me, Christ before me, Christ behind me, Christ in me, Christ beneath me, Christ above me, Christ on my right, Christ on my left, Christ in breadth, Christ in length, Christ in height, Christ in the heart of every man who thinks of me, Christ in the mouth of every man who speaks of me, Christ in every eye that sees me, Christ in every ear that hears me.

I arise today through a mighty strength, the invocation of the Trinity, through belief in the Threeness, through confession of the Oneness of the Creator of creation.

Salvation is of the Lord. Salvation is of Christ. May Thy Salvation, O Lord, be ever with us. Amen.[6]

---

6. "The Lorica (The Deer's Cry), WorldPrayers.org, http://www.worldprayers. org/archive/prayers/invocations/i_arise_today_through_a_mighty.html, (accessed April 7, 2016).

April

Pet Day (April 11)

Dear God,

Thank You so much for our pet(s). We love them! Thank You for placing [pet's name] in our lives and in our home. We are grateful for our pet's tenderness, kindness, and loving companionship. We thank You that our pet(s) is a gift of You. May we always treat him/her with gentle hands, admiration, and love. We ask You to bless them with Your almighty protection, loving care, and contentment. Please provide our pet with a long and happy life. We pray that You would keep them free of hurt, harm, or danger. For as your words in Psalm 145:9 says, *"The Lord is good to all, and his mercy is over all that he has made."* Thank You, God that You truly are merciful and affectionate, and that You love all of Your wonderful creations including our pet (s). We love them, too, and thank You for Your concern for them—not even a sparrow drops to the ground without You knowing, Lord. In Jesus' holy name, we pray and trust. Amen!

Palm Sunday

Dearest Heavenly Father,

Thank You for sending Your precious Son, Jesus, to come into this world. On the day Jesus rode into Jerusalem on a donkey, we imagine the parade of joy through the street as worshippers laid palm leaves. We realize that gladness turned quickly into sorrow; the road led to dying painstakingly and tragically on a wooden cross. We can't imagine the suffering You went through for us, Lord; we can only bow now as we are Yours, Lord, and so we worship You and take time out to remember Your profound sacrifice for us as sinners. Strengthen us, O Lord, in substantial measure with the perseverance You have carried even in the face of death.

Help us to have courage as Christians to nurture those in need, even as we, too, may face trouble and darkness. Be with us, Lord, in our valleys, and enable us to seek You with pure heart, soul, and purpose, and with true joy, worshipping You. Hosanna in the highest! Thank You, Holy God! In Jesus' name, we seek and pray. Amen!

Good Friday

Holy God in Heaven,

Hallowed be Your name. We approach Your heavenly throne on this Good Friday, reflecting on the very nature of Your sacrifice for us as sinners. As we realize the extremity of the death of Your Son, Jesus Christ, on the cross, we rest in deep sorrow regarding the plight of the cross, where Jesus took away our sins and forgave us our iniquities. We are thankful, beyond measure, for Your unconditional love over us this Friday and for Your plan for us as followers to pick up our crosses and pursue You in absolute obedience, trust, hopefulness, and faith. As we do this, may we comprehend the depth of Your love, and may we share with You our unyielding love and devotion. In Jesus' love, we pray, amen.

Praise for Easter

Praise God!

Hallelujah; the Lord is risen! The Lord is risen indeed! Let us be thankful for this lovely Easter day when we can give praise to our awesome Father, the One who sent His Son to die for us on the cross, to take our place and to stand in the gap between life and death, hope and hopelessness, good and evil. Praise Jesus! We have everlasting life, allowing Jesus to fill our hearts, as we walk with Him in our day-to-day lives, giving Him honor. We trust in Him for an extraordinary life eternal in His heavenly kingdom. Amen.

Arbor Day (Last Friday in April)

Powerful Father and Bountiful Creator,

Thank You, Lord, on this Arbor Day, for Your glorious, colorful, and mighty creation. May we advocate in concern for Your land and foundation, for the beauty and natural environment You have gracefully placed all around us to be admired and respected. May we be diligent caretakers of our world's trees, shrubs, plants, and flowers. We endeavor to enact healthy tree-planting and agricultural development. May we represent Your creation with honor and dignity. May our roots be based entirely in You, Jesus, in whom we pray and trust. Thank You, Jesus! Amen!

May

National Foster Care Month

Dear Father,

Your Word says in John 14:18, *"I will not leave you as orphans; I will come to you."* According to this Scripture and promise we pray, Lord, for our nation's precious foster children. Lord, there are hundreds of thousands of them and You know them by name; they are Yours and Your love for them overflows. As our hearts break for them, we lift them to Your tender concern to place them in safe, happy homes. May they be well-cared for, fed, sheltered, and provided for with pure tenderness, guided with loving, faithful, and hands. May each one feel great worth in Your eyes and in the eyes of loved ones. May each one be adopted as forever children—that none will be abused, harmed, or hurt. Lord, we ask for Your greatest favor, purest hope, and abiding love to flow over them like a gentle river full of Your mighty peace. In Jesus' name we pray and trust, amen!

National Day of Prayer (1st Thursday in May)

Precious God, Powerful King, and Ruler of All Nations,

We approach You on behalf of our ailing country. We take time now to pray and meditate on Your Word which is the sword of the Spirit and the path to righteousness. For as 2 Chronicles 7:14 says, "*if my people who are called by my name humble themselves, and pray and seek my face and turn from their wicked ways, then I will hear from heaven and will forgive their sin and heal their land.*" May we rest upon this Word, exalting You in prayer and crying out for Your great mercy and transformation of all that lies within our nation. Touch the hearts of our leaders to open their minds to You as the mighty Rock. May Your wisdom, knowledge, and understanding prevail in their minds and comfort their spirits. Give them a new direction secured in Christ's holy name. Grant us, as one nation under God, the courage to reject anything that is evil or sinful in Your eyes as Your people. Enable us to follow You and Your plan closely, adhering to Your will for our homeland, communities, and societies. Help us to jointly inspire one another to walk the Jesus walk and talk using calm, serene tongues. May violence and all ill-will be reduced. May peace, prosperity, justice, and optimism reign. O Lord our God, please hear the plea of Your faithful servants who kneel before You on this day. We ask for many souls to be saved, for massive healing over our country, and for nothing less than Your incredible glory made manifest. In Jesus' awe-inspiring name, we humble ourselves and pray. Amen!

Mother's Day (2nd Sunday in May)

Almighty God,

Our Rock, our Map of life and purpose, we give You countless thanks for our family members. We thank You for all the moms, grandmas, aunts, and women who have blessed us with their sac-rificial love. Please, Lord, encourage their hearts and move them near to Your heart; Jesus; incline to them to Your understanding. Gift each of us with wisdom to walk with You and honor You all the days of our lives in respect, obedience, and pure admiration. Remind us to be patient and kind, living via Your words and ways, kneeling together each day in prayer and praise. Rise up and call us blessed as a family with joyful and serving hearts. Thank You, Jesus! Amen.

Memorial Day (Last Monday in May)

Dearest Heavenly Father,

Thank You for granting us the freedom as Americans to pursue our hopes and dreams in You. Help us to recollect daily the overwhelming sacrifice that our men and women of the military have tendered to keep our country free. Bless our sons and daughters as they are witnesses to this protection. Please keep our military close under the shadow of Your wing as they face dangers both internal and external. Cover them with Your feathers as You watch over them and give them the ability to face obstacles of the day. Be with the moms and dads of those who lost their lives in wars past. We pray for their peace and capability to face life with courage and hope anew. May they remember that blessed are those who mourn, for they shall be comforted. (See Matthew 5:4.) May the armed forces have all they need to accomplish their missions with diligence and gentle assurance. Remind them of Your enduring love and faithfulness. Thank You, Jesus! Amen.

June

International Children's Day (June 1)

Praise You, God, for the world's amazing children,
For their hearts of gold and their eyes of wonder,
For their minds of wit and their voices of thunder,

For the gentle hugs, precious faces, and tender touch,
For their adorable ways that we love so much.
We thank You, Jesus, for all the world's children.
Protect those who are suffering and may not know
The love of a Father who sets their hearts aglow.
Please intercede for those who are in harm's way.
Let theirs be a brighter, more peaceful, meaningful day.
For those who are orphans, may they soon have families
Filled with love and affection and Your yoke of ease.
May their lives be abundantly joyful, happy, and walking
In Your will and guidance, may their mouths be talking
Of prayer, laughter, and hopeful abiding. Praise Jesus
Forevermore for the children. May they always know Your
Love first, for *"Let the little children come to me, and
do not hinder them, for the kingdom of heaven
belongs to such as these"* (Matthew 19:14 NIV).

Ocean Day (June 8)

Thank You, God, for the awe-inspiring beauty of the ocean; for the gentle breeze that surrounds it, for the aqua-blue inspired waters; for the calm and serene bays of glistening white and tan sands; for the way it calls our name as we recognize it's created in Your glory; for the message it delivers us as we await the powerful backdrop of its sunset, a family building a sandcastle or two birds soaring together in flight. May many see Your magnificence in reflection as they gaze at the wide wonder of all Your beauty and creation.

Thank You, Holy God. Amen!

Father's Day (3rd Sunday in June)

Holy God, Powerful God, Blessed Father,

It's in Your love that You made us a family, and we thank You for being our heavenly Father, teacher, guide, and instructor of how we should act. We thank You for our dads, grandpas, uncles, and all other men who love, guide, and mentor us. Lord, we praise You for them, and we ask Your blessing upon them to be their Father even as they father us. We can't do it without You, so please, Lord, step before us and help us to know how to accomplish our important family roles with pure love, hope, responsibility, and bravery. Help us to know when to communicate, when to step back and listen, when to encourage, and when to give gentle hugs to show we care. Help us to connect with one another and with You, God—as our precious heavenly Father. It's in Jesus' holy and powerful name, we pray. Amen.

July

July 4th, Independence Day

Dear God,

We are so thankful for the liberties that You have given us, especially the freedom of everlasting life—this we choose through Your precious Son, Jesus Christ. Thank You for the sacrifice Jesus made on the cross for all our sins. Thank You for the magnificent example Jesus provided with His life. Help us to never take that leadership for granted. Allow us to comprehend it, abide in it, and follow Jesus all the days of our lives. Thank You for the men and women who have bravely served our country, helping to ensure our freedoms and protecting our families, our homes, and our futures. Bless their lives with peace, comfort, safety, and security in all they do. Help them to return to their families if they are still deployed. Keep their bodies and souls out of harm's way. Let Your glory be known through their lives and ours as we serve You. Thank You, Jesus. Amen.

August

Back-to-School

Powerful God,

Thank You, God, for this time of returning to school and renewing our minds. May this be a year of joy and discovery. May we focus well on our studies and accomplish much in our grades and environment. May we never experience bullying or hopelessness, but only true friendship, peace, pure-hearted achievement, and success. May our schools be safe from any and all terrorism or plots of the enemy. May our teachers, principals, administration, and leaders be strong and capable. May our minds be expanded with vast knowledge and gentle assurance. We thank You, Jesus, for all Your good gifts. Praise You, Jesus, forevermore!

September

Labor Day (1st Monday in September)

Dear Heavenly Father,

We thank You and praise You, Holy God, for this Labor Day! Thank You, God, for allowing time to dwell in peace and rediscover the wonders of life. We claim Your promise that Your presence will go before us and give us rest. (See Exodus 33:14.) May we experience reassurance, bright sunshine, happiness, love, and peaceful moments as we regroup as a family. In the name of Your Son, who gives us this critical rest and relaxation, thank You, Holy God. Amen!

International Day of Peace (September 21)

O Lord of Peace,

On this day of peace, we lift to You the lives of all people on the face of this planet, all of whom are made in Your image, and we pray over them Philippians 4:7: "[May] *the peace of God, which surpasses all understanding...guard* [their] *hearts and* [their] *minds in Christ Jesus.*" May anxious thoughts and weary hearts be uplifted. May angry and impatient souls be calmed. May spirits be blessed with peace, unity, thoughts of You, and love. May all evil, all strongholds of the devil, and all troubles of darkness be gone in Jesus' holy name. May hopes be lifted and may we see nations united, arms in agreement, societies living in harmony, and, most of all, families acting in tranquility and goodness. May wars cease, worries be driven away, and harm and abuse be erased from our presence and our world's existence. May we experience quality time together. May we all act according to God's peaceful, plentiful, and good nature, according to Your lavish will for our lives; it's in Jesus' blood that we pray and trust. May this all be for Your purpose, plan, and marvelous glory. Praise Jesus! Amen.

October

Breast Cancer Awareness Month [A Blessing]

Precious women of hope, women who have suffered cancer, our friends, prayer partners, most trusted fellows and sisters in Christ, encouraging souls—you make us want to lead a more fulfilling, caring, serving, and deeper life in Christ.

Praise God for your courage! We pray now for you to hold on together and with Christ even when it hurts—and we know that sometimes it really, really hurts.

May you cling to Christ through the ups and downs; may you know He can and will heal you...because He loves you—you are the apple of His eye! He's with you in defeating this terrible disease. Our prayer is for you to fully overcome and to never face the disease ever again and to lead a fruitful, happy, healthy life.

We pray that you would know that Christ *inside* you is so much stronger than any cancer can ever be; it must go *now* from your body and you are free. We pray you will be totally free and healed indeed!

For our dear ones who have loved ones suffering—although we may not know them, we pray that they, too, will be healed, because God has made you, dear ones, some of the strongest, most beautiful people we know in this world...and we love you. We see God shining through you.

We pray for you and your loved ones, with all our hearts and souls, to be healed as true victors and champions for Christ, for you are loved, now and forevermore! In Christ's holy and precious name we trust.

Halloween (October 31)

Heavenly Father,

Bless us, Lord, deep in our beings. Protect our minds, bodies, and souls as we seek out entertainment this Halloween season. Help us to be safe and focused on Your good will and nothing less. Fill our views with love for humanity. Keep us free of any and all temptations, and lead us to the road that is everlasting. Give us a wonderful time of laughter and friendship. Be with us as we represent You each day, especially during this day, Halloween. Empower us to be Your light in the darkness. Thank You, Jesus! Amen.

November

Election Season

Thank You, Lord God, for the ability and freedom to choose our leaders. As Election Day approaches, please help us to have the pure wisdom and understanding to know the best candidates to fill these open positions in our government. Help us to choose good, godly candidates who will bless the people they govern. Enable us to be conscientious citizens who make faithful, honorable choices. Enable us to be subject to governing authorities as it says in Romans 13, and guide us toward peace, not division. Open our eyes to see anything that is false in the speeches and ideas that surround this election. We pray now for truth, for justice, and for candidates who will carry out Your will, God, and not their own. Thank You, Jesus! Amen.

Veteran's Day (November 11)

Dear Loving Father,

We read in Your Word in 1 Peter 4:12–14:*"Beloved, do not be surprised at the fiery trial when it comes upon you to test you, as though something strange were happening to you. But rejoice insofar as you share Christ's sufferings, that you may also rejoice and be glad when his glory is revealed. If you are insulted for the name of Christ, you are blessed, because the Spirit of glory and of God rests upon you."* Lord, many of our veterans have suffered deeply in fiery trials and tragic circumstances just as it says in 1 Peter. We plead Your greatest mercy over them to enable them to see Your joy restored again in their lives and in their family home. Cause them, Lord, to feel Your hand rest upon them. May they feel Your grace healing their souls and encouraging them to rejoice and be glad in the presence of Your genuine love. We praise You, Jesus, forevermore. Amen.

National Children's Day [A Blessing] (Nov. 20)

For the kids in our country's children's homes and in foster care: may God bless you and assure you of your great importance and worth, of His powerful and undeniable love over you in every moment of life, and of His very heart beating in you, His creation, and your mark on this world. You are a gift! May God bless you and shine His all-encompassing light and love on you.

For our kids and the children of our world with parents, grandparents, and guardians, may your hearts be warmed and held close by the loving arms of your family, fearlessly learning about life, growing, filling your minds with school, friends, hopefulness, goals, plans, fun, joy, toys, a future. With Christ at the center, may that future be bright and lovely, may your present *now* be spent discovering more and more each day His great and abiding love over you. For you are special, treasured, important, and adored by your Father in heaven and by your family here on earth.

We pray a critical blessing that the blood of Christ will cover every single child; may you each know that you are safe, that you are protected. May your minds be filled with wisdom, joy, peace, and love. May God's divine safeguard surround you and His comfort assure you both now and always, in Jesus' holy name, we trust.

National Adoption Day (Sat. before Thanksgiving)

Heavenly Father,

We offer You thanks, all-powerful King, for the gift of adoption. We enter Your gates with thanksgiving and we praise and bless You for Your precious orphan children having forever homes that You built—we know that You and You alone are the Cornerstone of our families. We ask that more and more orphans will be discovered, cherished, and adopted by Your chosen ones. We thank You for every soul involved in the adoption process. We pray for saved lives, rescued children, and united comforts of home. Praise Jesus now and always. Amen!

Thanksgiving (4th Thursday in November)

Dearest Father,

Our God, our hope, our liveliness, our purpose—You are the one influence in our lives that matters. We give You countless thanks today for all You are doing in our lives. Thank You for this very day that's a clear opportunity to give You honor and praise. Thank You for your bountiful provision: for food, for shelter, for sleep, for each other, for protection, for fun, for consistency, and for surprises. Thank You for never leaving us nor forsaking us, but instead always being at our right hand and at our left. We thank You and praise You for all You do and for who You are to us—our Prince of Peace who reigns in darkness; thank You, Jesus! Amen.

December

Advent

"Set your hope fully upon the grace that will be brought to you at the revelation of Jesus Christ" (1 Peter 1:13).

May Advent be a blessed time of preparation for the Christmas season.

May our anticipation find fulfillment in Christ alone.

May our hope lie in the hands of the trusted Lord who saves us.

May our joy be fulfilled by a sunny and beautiful tomorrow.

May our holiday traditions embody the meaning of His sacrifice.

May our spiritual peace exemplify the remarkable gift of Christ's love.

May we and our loved ones be protected from any anxieties and troubles.

May the concerns of our hearts be lifted in this prayer.

May we serve the Lord diligently with refreshed minds and rested hearts.

May we live in unity with all of our brothers and sisters in Christ.

May light fill our souls, our home, our family, and our future.

May we graciously accept the gift of grace given through Jesus Christ.

In Jesus Christ our Lord's precious and powerful name we pray, Amen.

Christmas Day (December 25)

Thank You, Lord, for another Christmas season, for humbling Yourself to become a Child here on earth so that You could grow, love, minister, and ultimately die on the cross for our sins. May Your light illuminate the path of a significant season of sharing and giving, with courage to move past simple traditions and give hope to those in need, give moments that we will all treasure, give glory to Your holy name, and give true joy in our experiences.

We pray for You to hold us near as we are grateful for the reason behind the season;

For faith to encourage our spirits, providing inspiration for our family each day;

For love in our home, peace in our relationships, revelations for the future;

For a shiny new year to be just around the bend as we prepare for Your work;

For compassionate remembrance of orphans and others in our world who need our aid;

For our family to delight in completeness and love from the One who first loved us;

For God's glory to be known through our charitable actions for others;

For a Christmas celebration and fulfillment in our hearts that will remain forever;

Thank You, Jesus!

Amen.

Special Occasions

A New Engagement

Dear Heavenly Father,

We thank *You*, Lord, for this important engagement. We approach You with pure bliss and thanksgiving on behalf of this loving couple. Thank You for the commitment between them as they plan to join lives together in holy matrimony, and for the affection they share. Thank You for their belief in everlasting love as they unite as one. Thank You for the adoration that has blossomed between them. May there be an unconditional love between them that safeguards a deep and abiding friendship. As they approach the wedding ceremony, may they live, love, and laugh with full and happy hearts. Offer them grace to listen to one another attentively. Be with them in their relationship and craft a spiritual bond that lasts forever. Please, Lord, be at the center of this marriage. Be the tree that stands tall, strong, and true with branches that will shelter this couple forever. Thank You, Jesus! Amen.

A Wedding

Dear God,

Our Father, our Creator, our Uniter—we lift to You this precious bond of marriage that is being formed between these two. We present their relationship before You, requesting Your almighty blessing and outpouring of love and faith upon them all the days of their lives. May they entrust their souls to You in assurance that You will guide them and enable them to love one another like You love us, that they will love You most of all as their one true Cornerstone for all eternity. May they be surrounded by a loving community to whom they can turn in the difficult days, but may they also form an unshakeable community in their home: a family that follows You. Allow their marriage to last in worship and celebration of You each and every moment of their partnership in Jesus Christ. Thank You, Jesus! Amen.

One's Anniversary

Loving Father,

Thank You for the incredible connection we have through marriage. Thank You for our deep abiding love, hope, and happiness together. Bless You, Lord Jesus, for the family we have developed in Your love. Thank You for a hopeful spirit between us that helps us look forward to many joyful, healthy, and plentiful years ahead despite hardships. Bless our children and our children's children with all the provisions of Your greatest prosperity and livelihood as they live out their days in service to You! Thank You, Jesus! It's in Your holy name we pray and trust. Amen.

A Newborn Baby

Dear God,

Thank You, Lord, that You gave this most cherished wonder of a child, a little life that is entrusted into the parents' hands to care for, hope for, dream for, and love. Thank You, God, that this child was knitted by Your holy hands, with purpose, direction, talents, and spiritual gifts that only this child can exhibit for Your kingdom, glory, honor, and missions. Thank You, Jesus, that life is truly a gift that You have molded and sent into the world for us to nurture and treasure. May the parents be the best they can possibly be with Your hands to guide them each day. Amen.

A Graduate

Holy and Faithful God,

Thank You for this day that is set before us, a day of graduation, a moment of honor, a time of praise, to say thank You for this graduate who entrusts his/her life and future to You. Focus them on Your path, show them the way to success and real inner peace. May his/her experiences and life produce abundant fruit for Your kingdom, in Jesus' mighty name, we pray. Thank You for a good education and opportunity to represent You, Jesus, in this cold and callous world. May he/she discover the truth that all contentment lies in a close, interwoven relationship with You, in walking with You from day to day, in listening for Your voice, Your power, Your commands, and in Your great love. Thank You Jesus! May it be so! In Your precious name we trust. Amen.

A Baptism

Dear Heavenly Father,

We thank You for Your Holy Spirit that is upon us in this baptism ceremony. May this ceremony be a symbol of faith, security, and unshakable trust. May Your love flow as the baptism honors You, knowing You have called Your sheep to follow Your influential voice, leading us and showing us the way. Surround us in Your hopefulness, Your bold protection, Your authority and glory today and forevermore. Fill us with Your Holy Spirit and enable all that surround this ceremony to be blessed by the blood of Jesus Christ, growing closer to You and the knowledge of Your holy presence and love. Thank You, Jesus! It's in Your mighty name, Jesus Christ, that we pray. Amen.

An Adoption

Dearest Heavenly Father,

Our God, our Rock, our King, our Provider, we thank You first that You adopted us into Your divine family and welcomed us into Your presence. Thank You also for this wonderful family about to adopt a blessed child. May the adoption go perfectly without any red tape or unforeseen trouble. Please put Your hedge of protection around this family, ensuring their needs are met—financially, spiritually, physically, and emotionally—as they prepare for this new child becoming a permanent addition to their home. We are so grateful for Your influence in providing necessary resources, moving the mountains, and ensuring all goes smoothly. We pray for miraculous bonding between the parents, child, and siblings/extended family/friends. We pray this family will feel Your hand uniting them in pure love and devotion. Please Lord, let it be so in Jesus' holy name. Amen.

A Birthday

Faithful King,

We thank You for another magnificent birthday! We rejoice in this day You have created, giving _____ life. For that and for so many reasons we are wholeheartedly grateful. Thank You for the marvelous memories this day brings for _____. Thank You for the people who have surrounded _____ with love. Thank You for Your divine and tremendous presence in our lives. As Psalm 139:14 says, *"I praise you, for I am fearfully and wonderfully made."* Even before _____ was born, You loved him/her with *agape*, pure, extraordinary love, and You love him/her that way still today. We pray that You would graciously watch over, guide, and care for _____ in the year ahead. Thank You for the love that You freely gave this past year, for Your watchful care over our family in good times and in bad. Thank You for bringing us together for this special and significant day. May this be the best birthday _____ has ever had, and may You receive all the credit and honor for the hope, joy, and peace You bring to our family. For it's in and through Jesus Christ, Your Son, that we pray. Amen!

A Housewarming

Dear God, Lord of all Creation, and Father,

We petition You today for a sacred blessing over this house. Thank You for the refuge it is for this family. May You quickly turn this house into a home. May it be a place of joy and laughter, may it be a place where You are cheerfully worshiped and served; may the family here always affirm, *"But as for me and my house, we will serve the* LORD*"* (Joshua 24:15). This is our prayer and our wish. And with that hope comes a request for only light and love to come into this dwelling, for no darkness or evil to be ever allowed here. Protect its entrance; allow only good to come through its doors. May happy and healthy relationships thrive within its walls, particularly this family's relationship with You, Lord. May each room be a meaningful space filled with love. May each person who enters this home feel welcome, feel Your power, and feel this family's adoration of You. May this home be a calm, quiet, and complete refuge for those who need rest. Refresh each body that lives within this home. May the hospitality of the saints be shown in these rooms. Let compassion, companionship, and a special warmth surround every member of this home, this family, and its neighbors. May Your Holy Spirit dwell within these walls and each of these important souls within, confirmed by Your richest blessings. In Jesus' holy name we pray and trust. Amen!

New Grandparents

Powerful, Loving Father,

We thank You today for giving us the gift of family. It's such a beautiful joy when someone is first a parent, and it's a crowning glory when somebody is made a grandparent. We thank You for the support of our new grandparents because they are cherished gifts to each of us. We pray Your mercy to watch over and protect these important souls. We recognize the power of Your love over them to guide them in their significant role in our lives. We cheerfully affirm with You a distinct blessing over their lives, livelihood, health, and future. May their strength be a role model to their grandchildren, steering them in peace, tradition, and love. May the notable witness of their faith be pillars of hope within the family now and forever more. May they live long, healthy, happy, and blessed lives, realizing the full crown of glory of this gift of a grandchild. May love flow abundant and true, in Jesus' almighty name, we seek and believe! Amen!

Finding a New Job

Sovereign God and King, Gracious and Loving Father,

We come now seeking You for divine favor over our family and our financial stability. As You have loved us with a powerful and everlasting love, we are in a critical phase now. We reach out for Your help and rescue, Lord, to ensure vast provision over our family. We are in a predicament of searching for a new job. We know You call us to provide and care for our families and others under our care. We can't do this without You, Lord, so we seek You. We ask for Your heavenly wisdom to direct us to Your abundant blessing of income, to coordinate for us the perfect job at the best possible timing within the ideal company, and to unite gifts and talents with an organization that will value and respect them completely. Please provide all the benefits, vacation time, retirement, insurance, and amenities that will make this happy employment. We ask for the job to be fruitful and multiply in vast proportion, with our assurance of providing more tithing for Your essential kingdom work and purposes. We commit to You and to the prospective employer hard work, dedication, trust, and loyalty. We strive to work as though we are serving You directly, Lord Jesus Christ. May our labors reveal to others our joy in You. Please Lord, come and arrange for us this valuable opportunity—a door opened, a position filled, a pleased company with a truly favored, rewarded employee. Let Your name be above all names. Amen!

Starting a New Job

Lord, there's no one like You. Our God, our Savior, our Rescuer, our Mighty King, thank You for this new job that is a true blessing of Your construction. We thank You for an open door no man can shut, for delivery in a time of certain need, for Your watch-care over our home, family, income, and future. May we follow You and Your expectations for our service in this new position. We recognize, God, that whether this is our dream job or the opposite, You knew what we needed precisely at the right time, ensuring the precise opportunity with a bright and meaningful future. May we serve our boss according to Your loyal measure. May we offer our best, faithful labor in full obedience. May Your favor be known power-fully through this job and all the future entails. May we partner in good graces with our coworkers and offer the best of Christ within us. May goals and dreams be fulfilled in and through You. May we tithe and bless Your plans for Your church and ministry. May Your name, Jesus, be glorified now and through the end of time for this job. Praise You, Jesus Christ, forever! Amen.

A New Retirement

Dearest Father God,

Our hope for a period of rest has been on Your shoulders; thank You for leading us/our family member to retirement. Thank You for the privilege it is to take moments to smell the roses, which You have graced us in Your gardens of truth and plenty. O Lord, we are excited about the retirement and what it will hold. May each minute of it be filled with actions and thoughts that bring hope to others and glory to You. May Your name, Jesus Christ, be exalted in all the lands for all eternity. May we charitably serve and wor-ship You in more compelling, impactful ways during this retire-ment phase. In Jesus' holy name we pray and trust. Amen!

A New Pregnancy

Heavenly Father and Creator,

Thank You for Your grand design of this new child grow-ing inside the womb, full of life, a beloved soul that matters so immensely to our family. May this baby be healthy and safe in the womb. Guard and protect this new life and the mom who carries this blessed child. May Mom be in divine health and energy throughout this pregnancy. May the baby be delivered at full-term—secure and sound in all of Your grace, with ideal timing and jubilation. May this child enter our lives as a part of a stable, peaceful, loving, and happy environment. Lord, we ask especially that this precious soul be filled with Your great love, hopefulness, destiny, and purpose, guiding him or her along the way in all of Your magnificence, mighty, devoted, generous, and triumphant King Jesus. Thank You, Jesus! Amen.

WHAT GOD SAYS ABOUT PRAYER

The Bible talks a lot about prayer! It is self-evident that prayer is supposed to be an important—a *vital*—part of the believer's life. To illuminate your family's understanding of prayer, I've gathered a few Scripture verses below, and roughly divided them into four sections, although of course there is much overlap between them: The Reason for Prayer, How to Pray, What We Should Expect from Prayer, Examples of Prayers in the Bible, and Praying by Topic. You can use these references as a springboard for your own study, especially with the help of a trusted commentary or study guide.

The Reason for Prayer

Psalm 23:4	Acts 2:42
Psalm 50:15	Acts 12:12
Psalm 55:22	Acts 20:36
Psalm 91:1–6, 14–16	1 Thessalonians 5:16–18
Psalm 103:1–5	1 Timothy 2:1
Jeremiah 29:11–14	James 1:5
Matthew 26:36	James 5:16

How to Pray

Genesis 18:27

2 Chronicles 7:14

Psalm 141:2

Proverbs 28:9

Matthew 6:7–13

Matthew 7:1–5

Matthew 21:6

Luke 18:1–5

Romans 8:26

1 Corinthians 1:4

Ephesians 6:18

Philippians 1:3–4

Philippians 4:1–5

Colossians 1:3

1 Timothy 2:5

1 Timothy 2:8

Hebrews 10:19–22

James 1:5–7

James 4:3

James 5:13–14

1 Peter 5:7

What We Can Expect from Prayer

Daniel 6:18–22

Isaiah 41:10

Isaiah 65:24

Matthew 21:21–22

Luke 11:9

John 14:13–14

John 16:26–27

Acts 10:9

Acts 12:5

Acts 16:25–26

2 Corinthians 12:7–9

2 Thessalonians 1:11

1 John 1:9

1 John 3:22

1 John 5:14–15

Examples of Prayers in the Bible

Amos 1:1–5

Amos 3:5–9

Psalm 27:1–5

Psalm 35:1–5

Psalm 41:1–4   Luke 11:1–4

Psalm 51:1–6   Acts 4:23–27

Daniel 9:1–5

Praying by Topic

This section contains a list of Scripture verses that can be used to pray over specific needs or topics. If you are a position of need, locate one of these Scriptures to pray over and pray through. It's when we pray God's words back to Him that we find our wills aligning with His will on the issue at hand.

For: decisions about the future, about work, business, parenting, marriage, college, school, careers, or health; lack of wisdom, uncertainty, loss of direction, cry for help.

Pray: *"Call to me and I will answer you, and will tell you great and hidden things that you have not known"* (Jeremiah 33:3).

For: Doubt, concerns, frustrations, loneliness, discouragement, finances, revelations, fear, grief, anger.

Pray: *"Before they call I will answer; while they are yet speaking I will hear"* (Isaiah 65:24).

"Likewise the Spirit helps us in our weakness. For we do not know what to pray for as we ought, but the Spirit himself intercedes for us with groanings too deep for words" (Romans 8:26).

For: Our nation, world, community, peace, humility, evil, natural disasters, storms, missions work.

Pray: *"If my people who are called by my name humble themselves, and pray and seek my face and turn from their wicked ways, then I will hear from heaven and will forgive their sin and heal their land"* (2 Chronicles 7:14).

For: The homeless, needy, poor, underprivileged, family and friend relationships, marriage, parenting, forgiveness.

Pray: "And Jesus answered them, 'Have faith in God. Truly, I say to you, whoever says to this mountain, "Be taken up and thrown into the sea," and does not doubt in his heart, but believes that what he says will come to pass, it will be done for him. Therefore I tell you, whatever you ask in prayer, believe that you have received it, and it will be yours. And whenever you stand praying, forgive, if you have anything against anyone, so that your Father also who is in heaven may forgive you your trespasses'" (Mark 11:22–26).

For: Waiting, uncertainty, the in-between spots in life, perseverance, patience, persistence, resolve, ongoing battles.

Pray: "And he told them a parable to the effect that they ought always to pray and not lose heart. He said, 'In a certain city there was a judge who neither feared God nor respected man. And there was a widow in that city who kept coming to him and saying, "Give me justice against my adversary." For a while he refused, but afterward he said to himself, "Though I neither fear God nor respect man, yet because this widow keeps bothering me, I will give her justice, so that she will not beat me down by her continual coming."' And the Lord said, 'Hear what the unrighteous judge says. And will not God give justice to his elect, who cry to him day and night? Will he delay long over them? I tell you, he will give justice to them speedily'" (Luke 18:1–8).

For: Calling, vocation, destiny, purpose in life, life's meaning, career goals, mid-life crisis, new situations.

Pray: "You did not choose me, but I chose you and appointed you that you should go and bear fruit and that your fruit should abide, so that whatever you ask the Father in my name, he may give it to you" (John 15:16).

For: Fear, doubt, disbelief, uncertainty, questions, fear, temptations.

Pray: "And I tell you, ask, and it will be given to you; seek, and you will find; knock, and it will be opened to you. For everyone who asks *receives, and the one who seeks finds, and to the one who knocks it will be opened"* (Luke 11:9–10).

For: Dreams, goals, hopes, plans, excitement, inspiration, future-looking, anticipation, celebration.

Pray: *"If you abide in me, and my words abide in you, ask whatever you wish, and it will be done for you"* (John 15:7).

Just Remember...

When you pray, God moves.

It may take time. God's time! Yet, as God works, great things happen.

He is an incredible and loving God.

He deserves our praise, honor and spoken glory.

The Lord cherishes our focus on prayer, especially when we do so as a family. This is our way to communicate with a powerful, faithful Father. So, how about it? Pray now! Seek God with your family's combined hearts. Make your family's prayer life come alive.

CLASSIC CHILDREN'S PRAYERS

As parents, do you remember the old classic prayers you were taught growing up? I can still remember our family prayer that we delivered daily: "God is good, God is great; let us thank Him for our food."

Here are some prayers that might bring back memories for you. They are a resource to use with your children as the occasion arises. They carry a "Use with Caution" label, because children should always remember that they can use their own words to talk with God whenever they want. However, sometimes a memorized prayer to recite at night or over food is very helpful for children. I also sprinkled some new prayers throughout to remind and encourage you that God is always creating new things in our families.

Come Lord Jesus

Come Lord Jesus, be our guest,
Let this food to us be blessed, amen.
—*Traditional*

Now I Lay Me Down to Sleep

Now I lay me down to sleep,
I pray the Lord my soul to keep;

If I die before I wake,
I pray for Lord my soul to take. Amen.[7]

Thank You, God, for Everything

Thank You for the world so sweet,
Thank You for the food we eat.
Thank You for the birds that sing,
Thank You, God, for everything.
—*Author Unknown*

God Is Great

God is great!
God is good!
Let us thank Him
For our food.
Amen.
—*Traditional*

The Lord's Prayer

Our Father, which art in heaven,
Hallowed be thy name.
Thy kingdom come,
Thy will be done in earth, as it is in heaven.
Give us this day our daily bread.
And forgive us our debts, as we forgive our debtors.
And lead us not into temptation, but deliver us from evil:
For thine is the kingdom, and the power, and the glory, for ever.
Amen. (Matthew 6:9–13 KJV)

---

7. *New-England Primer*, originally published in 1690 by Boston: Benjamin
Harris, Boston; this version is from a 1777 edition published by Massachusetts
Sabbath School Society in 1843, and now available at www.sacred-texts.com/
chr/nep/ (accessed April 7, 2016).

Serenity Prayer

God grant me the serenity
To accept the things I cannot change;
Courage to change the things I can;
And wisdom to know the difference.
—*Reinhold Niebuhr*

The Irish Blessing

May the road rise to meet you,
May the wind be always at your back,
May the sun shine warm upon your face,
The rains fall soft upon your fields and until we meet again,
May God hold you in the palm of His hand.
—*Anonymous*

Believer's Prayer

Lord, I believe You are the Creator of the universe,
The Helper of the poor, the Molder of the weak,
The Purpose of our existence, the Future of our lives.
Shape us to be Your faithful followers,
Help us to be more like You—
Loving, kind, forgiving, hopeful, and true.
Work through our lives to bring Your greatest glory through
our family and existence.
Thank You, Jesus!
Amen.
—*Teresa J. Herbic*

Twenty–Third Psalm

The Lord is my shepherd; I shall not want.
He makes me lie down in green pastures.

He leads me beside still waters.
He restores my soul.
He leads me in paths of righteousness for his name's sake.
Even though I walk through the valley of the shadow of death,
I will fear no evil, for you are with me;
Your rod and your staff, they comfort me.
You prepare a table before me
In the presence of my enemies;
You anoint my head with oil;
My cup overflows.
Surely goodness and mercy shall follow me
All the days of my life,
And I shall dwell in the house of the LORD *forever.*

God Is Close

God is close, God is near,
God is good, so never fear.
God is working, God is true,
God is hope, God is our glue!
—Teresa J. Herbic

Prayer of Common Worship

Gracious God, our sins are too heavy to carry, too real to hide, and too deep to undo. Forgive what our lips tremble to name, what our hearts can no longer bear, and what has become for us a consuming fire of judgment. Set us free from a past that we cannot change; open to us a future in which we can be changed; and grant us grace to grow more and more in Your likeness and image, through Jesus Christ, the light of the world. Amen. [8]

---

8. *PCUSA Book of Common Worship* (Louisville, KY: Westminster John Knox, 1993), 88.

The Prayer of Faith

God is my help in every need;
God does my every hunger feed;
God walks beside me, guides my way
Through every moment of this day.

I now am wise, I now am true,
Patient and kind, and loving, too;
All things I am, can do, and be,
Through Christ the Truth, that is in me.

God is my health, I can't be sick;
God is my strength, unfailing, quick;
God is my all, I know no fear,
Since God and Love and Truth are here.
—Hannah More Kohaus

I Behold the Christ in You

I behold the Christ in you,
Here is the life of God I see;
I can see a great peace too,
I can see you whole and free.

I behold the Christ in you.
I can see this as you walk;
I can see this in all you do,
I can see this as you talk.

I behold God's love expressed,
I can see you filled with power;
I can see you ever blessed,
See Christ in you hour by hour.

I behold the Christ in you,
I can see that perfect one;
Led by God in all you do,
I can see God's work is done.
—*Frank B. Whitney*

Martin Luther King Prayer

Thou Eternal God, out of whose absolute power and infinite intelligence the whole universe has come into being, we humbly confess that we have not loved thee with our hearts, souls, and minds, and we have not loved our neighbors as Christ loved us. We have all too often lived by our own selfish impulses rather than by the life of sacrificial love as revealed by Christ. We often give in order to receive. We love our friends and hate our enemies. We go the first mile but dare not travel the second. We forgive but dare not forget. And so as we look within ourselves, we are confronted with the appalling fact that the history of our lives is the history of an eternal revolt against you. But thou, O God, have mercy upon us. Forgive us for what we could have been but failed to be. Give us the intelligence to know your will. Give us the courage to do your will. Give us the devotion to love your will. In the name and Spirit of Jesus, we pray. Amen.
—*Dr. Martin Luther King*[9]

Make Me an Instrument of Your Peace

Lord, make me an instrument of your peace.
Where there is hatred, let me sow love,
Where there is injury, pardon.
Where there is doubt, faith.

---

9. Dr. Martin Luther King, Jr., "Thou, Dear God" (Boston: Beacon Press, 2011), ebook.

Where there is despair, hope.
Where there is darkness, light.
Where there is sadness, joy.
O Divine Master, grant that I may not so much
Seek to be consoled as to console,
Not so much to be understood as to understand,
Not so much to be loved, as to love;
For it is in giving that we receive,
It is in pardoning that we are pardoned,
It is in dying that we awake to eternal life.
—*St. Francis of Assisi*

Simple Prayer

God in heaven hear my prayer,
Keep me in Thy loving care.
Be my guide in all I do,
Bless all those who love me too.
Amen.
—*Traditional*

Bless Thy Bounty

Bless us, O Lord, and these Thy gifts which we are about to receive from Thy bounty, through Christ our Lord, amen.
—*Traditional*

Apostles' Creed

I believe in God, the Father Almighty, Creator of heaven and earth; and in Jesus Christ, His only Son, our Lord; Who was conceived by the Holy Spirit, born of the Virgin Mary, suffered under Pontius Pilate, was crucified, died, and was buried. He descended into hell; the third day He arose again from the dead. He ascended into heaven, and sits at the right hand of God, the Father Almighty; from thence He shall come to judge the living and the dead. I believe in the Holy Spirit, the holy catholic church, the communion of saints, the forgiveness of sins, the resurrection of the body and life everlasting. Amen.

A Silly Prayer

Rub-a-dub-dub,
Thanks for the grub.
Yay, God!
—*Author Unknown*

Psalm 121

I lift up my eyes to the hills. From where does my help come?
My help comes from the LORD, *who made heaven and earth.*
He will not let your foot be moved; he who keeps you will not slumber.
Behold, he who keeps Israel will neither slumber nor sleep.
The LORD *is your keeper; the* LORD *is your shade on your right hand.*
The sun shall not strike you by day, nor the moon by night.
The LORD *will keep you from all evil; he will keep your life.*
The LORD *will keep your going out and your coming in*
From this time forth and forevermore.

Father, We Thank Thee

Father, we thank thee for the night,
And for the pleasant morning light;
For rest and food and loving care,
And all that makes the day so fair.
Help us to do the things we should,

To be to others kind and good;
In all we do, in work or play,
To grow more loving every day.
—*Rebecca Weston, 1890*

A Mother's Cry

Dear God,
Thank You for the joy of being a mom,
I lift my children to You all day long.
Help them to be loving, positive, and kind,
Help them to be joyful and of sound mind.
Keep them far from evil plots and schemes.
Help them to succeed and fulfill their dreams.
Thank You, Jesus!
Amen.
—*Teresa J. Herbic*

A Father's Plea

Almighty Father in heaven,
Thank You for my family.
Praise You that You make them so sweet and fun.
Help them to shine like the noonday sun.
Gift them with Your special treasures of life,
Remind them it's not about money, worry, or strife.
Guide them to be more like You,
Assure them of all that is true.
Amen.
—*Galen D. Herbic*

A Child's Assignment

I'm on a mission for You, God.
To be a great leader for Your cause,

To know You are God and to be still,
All for Your reasons and good will.
To understand when to wait and when to act,
To realize that You always have my back.
To learn all that I need to know
To share my testimony with a real glow.
To look to the future through Your eyes,
To stay away from the devil and his lies.
To be an obedient child, I commit my path
Even when I don't know all of the math.
Thank You, God! In Jesus' holy name, I pray.
Amen.
—*Teresa J. Herbic*

Children's Mealtime Blessing

Thank You for the world so sweet,
Thank You for the food we eat.
Thank You for the birds that sing,
Thank You, God, for everything.
—*Author Unknown*

Child's Evening Prayer

I hear no voice, I feel no touch,
I see no glory bright;
But yet I know that God is near,
In darkness as in light.
He watches ever by my side,
And hears my whispered prayer:
The Father for His little child
Both night and day doth care.
—*Author Unknown*

Morning Prayer

I give thanks to you, heavenly Father, through Jesus Christ your dear Son, that you have protected me through the night from all danger and harm. I ask you to preserve and keep me, this day also, from all sin and evil, that in all my thoughts, words, and deeds I may serve and please you. Into your hands I commend my body and soul and all that is mine. Let your holy angels have charge of me, that the wicked one have no power over me.
Amen.
—Martin Luther

Evening Prayer

I give thanks to you, heavenly Father, through Jesus Christ your dear Son, that you have this day so graciously protected me. I beg you to forgive me all my sins and the wrong which I have done. By your great mercy defend me from all the perils and dangers of this night. Into your hands I commend my body and soul, and all that is mine. Let your holy angels have charge of me, that the wicked one have no power over me.
—Martin Luther

Father, We Honor You

Dearest Father God,
We honor You in all we do, we trust You in all things.
We hope for You in our comings and goings, we worship You in all ways.
Without You, we are nothing. With You, we have everything.
Thank You, Jesus! Amen.
—Teresa J. Herbic

The "Glory Be" Prayer (Gloria Patri)

Glory be to the Father, and to the Son, and to the Holy Spirit. As it was in the beginning, is now, and ever shall be, world without end.
Amen.

Praise God from Whom All Blessings Flow

Praise God, from whom all blessings flow;
Praise Him, all creatures here below;
Praise Him above, ye heav'nly host;
Praise Father, Son, and Holy Ghost!
Praise God the Father who's the source;
Praise God the Son who is the course;
Praise God the Spirit who's the flow;
Praise God, our portion here below!
—Thomas Ken

CONCLUSION:
FATHER'S LOVE LETTER

Read the following "Father's Love Letter" offered by our faithful partners at Father Heart Communications. As you read and absorb the Scriptures, think about how much God had you in mind when He created the world. He did everything out of His great love for you, His child. I hope that you and your family read this letter time and time again, and even consider creating your own family or individual "Love Letter to God," from your heart to His as mentioned in devotional 1. It's sure to be a meaningful and lasting experience!

Father's Love Letter—An Intimate Message from God to You.

My Child,

You may not know me, but I know everything about you. (Psalm 139:1)

I know when you sit down and when you rise up. (Psalm 139:2)

I am familiar with all your ways. (Psalm 139:3)

Even the very hairs on your head are numbered. (Matthew 10:29–31)

For you were made in my image. (Genesis 1:27)

In me you live and move and have your being, for you are my offspring. (Acts 17:28)

I knew you even before you were conceived. (Jeremiah 1:4–5)

I chose you when I planned creation. (Ephesians 1:11–12)

You were not a mistake, for all your days are written in my book. (Psalm 139:15–16)

I determined the exact time of your birth and where you would live. (Acts 17:26)

You are fearfully and wonderfully made. (Psalm 139:14)

I knitted you together in your mother's womb. (Psalm 139:13)

And brought you forth on the day you were born. (Psalm 71:6)

I have been misrepresented by those who don't know me. (John 8:41–44)

I am not distant and angry, but am the complete expression of love. (1 John 4:16)

And it is my desire to lavish my love on you. (1 John 3:1)

Simply because you are my child, and I am your Father. (1 John 3:1)

I offer you more than your earthly father ever could. (Matthew 7:11)

For I am the perfect father. (Matthew 5:48)

Every good gift that you receive comes from my hand. (James 1:17)

For I am your provider and I meet all your needs. (Matthew 6:31–33)

My plan for your future has always been filled with hope. (Jeremiah 29:11)

Because I love you with an everlasting love. (Jeremiah 31:3)

My thoughts toward you are countless as the sand on the seashore. (Psalm 139:17–18)

And I rejoice over you with singing. (Zephaniah 3:17)

I will never stop doing good to you. (Jeremiah 32:40)

For you are my treasured possession. (Exodus 19:5)

I desire to establish you with all my heart and all my soul. (Jeremiah 32:41)

And I want to show you great and marvelous things. (Jeremiah 33:3)

If you seek me with all your heart, you will find me. (Deuteronomy 4:29)

Delight in me and I will give you the desires of your heart. (Psalm 37:4)

For it is I who gave you those desires. (Philippians 2:13)

I am able to do more for you than you could possibly imagine. (Ephesians 3:20)

For I am your greatest encourager. (2 Thessalonians 2:16–17)

I am also the Father who comforts you in all your troubles. (2 Corinthians 1:3–4)

When you are brokenhearted, I am close to you. (Psalm 34:18)

As a shepherd carries a lamb, I have carried you close to my heart. (Isaiah 40:11)

One day I will wipe away every tear from your eyes. (Revelation 21:3–4)

And I'll take away all the pain you have suffered on this earth. (Revelation 21:3–4)

I am your Father, and I love you even as I love my Son, Jesus. (John 17:23)

For in Jesus, my love for you is revealed. (John 17:26)

He is the exact representation of my being. (Hebrews 1:3)

He came to demonstrate that I am for you, not against you. (Romans 8:31)

And to tell you that I am not counting your sins. (2 Corinthians 5:18–19)

Jesus died so that you and I could be reconciled. (2 Corinthians 5:18–19)

His death was the ultimate expression of my love for you. (1 John 4:10)

I gave up everything I loved that I might gain your love. (Romans 8:31–32)

If you receive the gift of my Son Jesus, you receive me. (1 John 2:23)

And nothing will ever separate you from my love again. (Romans 8:38–39)

Come home and I'll throw the biggest party heaven has ever seen. (Luke 15:7)

I have always been Father, and will always be Father. (Ephesians 3:14–15)

My question is…Will you be my child? (John 1:12–13)

I am waiting for you. (Luke 15:11–32)

Love,
Your Dad,
Almighty God[10]

----

10. "Father's Love Letter" used by permission of Father Heart Communications ©1999, FathersLoveLetter.com

I encourage you now to remember this *agape*—pure and honest—love that flows through God's Scriptures and this letter written to and for you as God's child. Go forth in consistent prayer with your family—your inner circle, and turn to the various prayer activities in this book whenever you need refreshing. May God truly bless you with His delight, inspiring you as you work with Him to safeguard and declare the success of your family's prayer life for Jesus Christ.

APPENDIX: PRAYER RESOURCES

About.com Christianity Web Channel

This informative site includes Christian prayers and Bible verses for specific areas of life to help you become more effective in your prayer life. It also provides a source for online prayer chains and networks where you can submit online prayer requests.

 christianity.about.com/od/prayersverses/

All About GOD Ministries, Inc.

This nonprofit, based in Colorado Springs, Colorado, creates websites that reach out to skeptics, seekers, believers, and a hurting world with powerful evidence for God and the good news of Jesus.

 allaboutgod.com/christian-prayer.htm

Back to the Bible

A worldwide Christian ministry dedicated to leading people into a dynamic relationship with Jesus Christ through Bible-based resources and teachings.

 backtothebible.org

Belief Net

Inspiring Christian prayers online to keep you strong in your faith and beliefs.

 beliefnet.com/Faiths/Prayer/Inspiring-Christian-Prayers.aspx

Billy Graham Evangelical Association (and Samaritan's Purse)

BGEA conducts regular crusades and prayer rallies throughout America and the world for Christ in which attendees can worship and pray with prayer partners. Samaritan's Purse partners with BGEA on events. They also conduct remarkable programs for children in need such as Operation Christmas Child and the Children's Heart Project.

 billygraham.org and samaritanspurse.org

Christian Broadcasting Network

CBN is a global ministry committed to preparing the nations of the world for the coming of Jesus Christ through mass media. Select the ministry's prayer tab online to find some great reference material, guidance sheets, and devotionals. You can also submit prayers regarding specific topics on your heart.

 www1.cbn.com/prayer

ChristianAnswers.net

Practical tips on praying with power, as well as important principles of prayer and answers as to why we should all seek God in prayer.

 christiananswers.net/q-comfort/growing-prayer.html

Christianity.com

A wealth of informative resources including tips for a meaningful prayer life, audio, text, video, and prayer to inspire and encourage you.

 christianity.com/christian-life/prayer/

Crossroads Prayer Line

Based in Canada, this organization loves to pray with callers and web connectors from all over the world. They provide a twenty-four hour prayer line full of love, compassion, comfort, and support for any prayer need.

 crossroads.ca/247prayer or call 866.273.4444.

Daystar

Christian television and broadcasting network focused on spreading the gospel seven days a week, twenty-four hours a day, worldwide. Offers prayer support.

 daystar.com or call 800.329.0029.

Dr. Tony Evans and the Urban Alternative

Great site where you can sign up for free inspirational ebooks, devotionals, prayer materials, and more.

 tonyevans.org

God's Own

God's Own is designed as a journey of personal discovery through prayer, worship, Bible study and important seeking activity. The course helps you to see yourself through the eyes of God. The Addict Whisperer is also part of God's Own, designed for those struggling with addiction and for those with loved ones who hurt.

 iamgodsown.com

Guideposts

Provides a prayer ministry where you can pray for others or submit your own prayer requests. Guideposts also produces regular daily devotionals and inspirational publications online and in print.

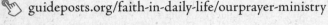 guideposts.org/faith-in-daily-life/ourprayer-ministry

Harvest Prayer Ministries

Full array of prayer resources for families, including praying for our country, prayer Scriptures, teaching guides, free downloads, and more. Also houses a prayer retreat center for those planning a God-centered getaway.

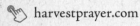 harvestprayer.com

Hope for the Heart

This organization specializes in heart care for those in deep need for healing of hurts, hang-ups, and difficult life trials. You can go online to hopefortheheart.org for powerful help and resources or call 800.488.HOPE for prayer and spiritual support.

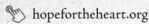 hopefortheheart.org

Joan Hunter Ministries

Prayer warriors who will pray with you about the needs of your heart. You will also find healing, prosperity, joy, and love Scriptures on this site to aid in your personal prayer journey.

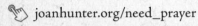 joanhunter.org/need_prayer

John Hagee Ministries

John Hagee Ministries offers amazing encouragement for worship, intercessory prayer, and direction in life. The entire Hagee family is part of the church's efforts. Their prayer ministry provides incredible prayer support online and by phone for those in need.

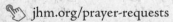 jhm.org/prayer-requests

Kenneth Copeland Ministries

Ministry that works hard to build up believers through faith, prayer, and spiritual growth opportunities.

 kcm.org.

Kerry Shook Ministries

Offers solid and regular prayer support to its friends, callers, and partners. Simply go online to submit a request at kerryshook.org/prayer-request or contact their prayer line by calling 866.226.9866.

 kerryshook.org/prayer-request

KLove

Christian radio station with a great prayer team to pray over your online-submitted prayer requests. You can also contact their care team via telephone at 800.525.5683.

 klove.com/ministry/prayer

LeSea Prayer Line

Powerful group of prayer warriors who will pray over your heart's cries day and night. Website offers a prayer request submission, a prayer wall, and encouraging thoughts.

 lesea.com/prayerline or call 800.365.3732.

Moody Radio

Moody Radio offers programs filled with sound biblical insight, communicating the message of God to listeners.

 moodyradio.org

National Day of Prayer (first Thursday in May)

The mission of the National Day of Prayer Task Force is to mobilize prayer in America and to encourage personal repentance and righteousness in the culture. Its website provides information about prayer activities in your area.

 nationaldayofprayer.org

National Pastors' Prayer Network

Not just for pastors, this site connects people to God through corporate prayer, and offers many learning opportunities such as online articles, blogs, and a list of pastor prayer groups across the country.

 nppn.org

Praise FM

Christian radio station with a special prayer wall on their website for anyone to ask for or contribute prayers of support to others.

 praisefm.org/prayer/

Prayer Resources, Inc.

Christian prayer ministry that offers some great, relatable personal stories and testimonies about prayer.

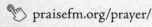 prayerresources.org

Prayer Stream, Christian Care Ministry

Christian Care Ministry uses social media to connect believers to each other, so that they can encourage one another and come together to praise and pray to God.

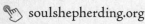 mychristiancare.org/prayerstream/prayerstream_landing_page.aspx

Soul Shepherding

Amazing prayer and Bible study resources for families, community groups, and small groups.

 soulshepherding.org

T. D. Jakes Ministries

Offers worship, praise and prayer conferences as well as an online prayer form for submitting personal prayer requests.

 tdjakes.org

The Upper Room Living Prayer Center

Open seven days a week, the center intercedes for callers and online visitors regularly in focused prayer. The Upper Room website offers resources for small groups, spirituality, and special e-learning opportunities about God and prayer.

 prayer-center.upperroom.org/ or call 800.251.2468.

Train and Grow

Digital home of all the ministry resources of Cru's US Campus Ministry (USCM)—well-organized website with free reading material, and free videos to watch, listen, download, or share.

 cru.org/train-and-grow.html

Trinity Broadcasting Network (TBN)

A praise and prayer line for seekers who need to find Jesus. You can go online to www.tbn.org to submit a request or to view great testimonies and messages about the Lord Jesus Christ.

 www.tbn.org

Woodrow Kroll Ministries

Offers Bible literacy resources, as well as great material about Psalms prayers—praise and thanksgiving from the book of Psalms. Woodrow Kroll is one of the all-time great Back to the Bible teachers who has communicated the importance of the Bible and led Christian messages of God's Word and prayer internationally.

 wkministries.com

World Day of Prayer

Held the first Friday in March, the World Day of Prayer is a worldwide movement of Christian women of many traditions who come together to observe a common day of prayer each year. It is a movement which brings together women of various races, cultures, and traditions in closer fellowship, understanding, and action throughout the year.

 worlddayofprayer.net.

ACKNOWLEDGMENTS

To Galen, Meyana, Braxten, and Lolli who share my passion for prayer and the Lord. To my extended family and church family who prayed with us unceasingly for miracles for both my son and daughter. To my family of prayer friends who stand with us in all of life's journeys. And as always, my heart goes out to the orphans of this world who need a home. May God truly bless you and bring you into His holy presence of the inner circle—family.

—Teresa J. Herbic

ABOUT THE AUTHOR

Teresa Herbic is adviser and cofounder of Families for Adoption, an international and domestic adoption, foster, and orphan care network based out of Pleasant Valley Baptist Church, Liberty, Missouri. She has published newspaper articles, two children's books about adoption, *Cat Tales* and *Dog Tales*, monthly articles for *Refocused Magazine*, and devotional writings for David C. Cook's *The Quiet Hour*. Herbic worked as creative director of an advertising agency and as a global market analyst/marketing manager for a major telecommunications firm. There, she became writer and editor of the company's weekly newsletter and operations manual. She later co-founded the company CAMP Relationships, LLC, hosting educational seminars and programs for family and marriage enrichment. She's a volunteer and faith writer for the Humane Society of the United States and a speaker for the Park University River Read Festival. She was the recipient of a Menn Thorpe Award for Literary Excellence Nominee in 2014 and 2015. God has blessed her and her husband, Galen, with two adopted children, Meyana and Braxten. They currently live in San Antonio, Texas.